The Life of Saint Paul

The

Life

of

Saint Paul

by

Harry Emerson Fosdick

Illustrated by Leonard Everett Fisher

THIS SPECIAL EDITION IS PRINTED AND DISTRIBUTED BY
ARRANGEMENT WITH THE ORIGINATORS AND PUBLISHERS
OF LANDMARK BOOKS *Random House, Inc.,* NEW YORK, BY

E. M. HALE AND COMPANY
EAU CLAIRE, WISCONSIN

© Copyright, 1962, by Harry Emerson Fosdick

All rights reserved under International and Pan-American Copyright Conventions. Published in New York by Random House, Inc., and simultaneously in Toronto, Canada, by Random House of Canada, Limited. Library of Congress Catalog Card Number: 62-7881 Manufactured in the United States of America Design by Jerome Kuhl

Contents

v

Author's Note

A book that tells the life story of Paul the Apostle raises one question from the start. Paul died about nineteen hundred years ago, after one of the most exciting, dangerous and influential lives ever lived. How, then, do we know so many details about what happened to him so long ago, about how he felt and what he did? The answer is twofold.

First, we have in the New Testament thirteen letters ascribed to Paul. While some scholars have doubted whether two or three of them were written by him, these letters furnish us with a great mass of first-hand, fascinating information. Then, second, we have in the New Testament *The Acts of the Apostles,* a book written by one of Paul's closest friends, Luke. Luke was a Gentile physician, and in our life story of Paul we shall have much to say about him. His book, *The Acts,* is written partly in the first person. He says "we" did so and so, because he was Paul's companion on some of his most important journeys. Other parts contain information about Paul and the early church which Luke learned from other people. These two sources, Paul's own letters and Luke's book, furnish us with the facts that make it possible to tell Paul's life story.

Grateful as we are for the information we do have, we are often disappointed because there are vacant places in the story. Again and again we feel like saying: "Please, Luke, tell us more about that!" To understand these omissions we must remember what it was like to write a book then. In Luke's time all books were written and copied by

Author's Note

hand, and a book was not made up of printed leaves of paper bound together. Instead it was written on rolls of papyrus, a water plant that grew in the valley of the Nile River. Out of its stem thin strips were cut. The crushed strips were then matted into sheets about a foot square. Twenty or thirty of these sheets, joined together, would make a long roll. The reader held this roll on his knees or laid it on a table, unwinding as he read. Because of this the length of books was limited. Actually Luke's book, *The Acts*, is one of the longest in the New Testament. Doubtless he often wanted to tell us more, but he had to compress his material to keep the long roll of papyrus from becoming unmanageable.

Nevertheless, we have a great deal of intimate, first-hand information about Paul's life, and it makes an interesting story.

H. E. F.

The Life of Saint Paul

I

Paul's Youth

When Jesus was about fifteen years old, living in his hometown of Nazareth in Palestine, a son was born to a Jewish family in Tarsus, a city more than three hundred miles to the northwest. Although we now know that son as Paul the Apostle, or Saint Paul, his family called him by a Hebrew name, Saul. Paulus was his Roman name.

Tarsus, at the time of Paul's birth, was a flourishing Greek city with probably half a million inhabitants. The capital of Cilicia in Asia Minor, it had a wonderful harbor, and it profited financially from the eastern trade route which there made contact with the Mediterranean. It was also famous for its university. Indeed one well-known writer of the time said that Tarsus as a center of learning was superior to both Athens and Alexandria.

Paul's early years, therefore, were very different from those of the youthful Jesus. Jesus was a country boy. His teaching is full of references which go back to his early life in the country—sheep and shepherds, seed time and harvest, trees and their fruit, hens and chickens, thorns and thistles, camels and foxes, oxen and asses. There is nothing like that in Paul's letters, which make up a large part of the New Testament. Paul, or Saul, was a city boy, and in his manhood his work was centered in the great cities of the Roman Empire. Once he quotes an ancient Jewish law, "You shall not muzzle an ox when it is treading out the grain," but that quotation is about the only expression of his which reminds the reader of country life.

In reading Paul's letters we find ourselves in one

city after another. And if he wants to illustrate a principle such as self-control, he seems naturally to think not of some country scene but of the big games in the amphitheaters. For instance he writes, "Every athlete exercises self-control in all things."

Paul had a sincere pride in his home city. Once when he was in grave danger and a Roman tribune was trying to find out who he was, he answered, "I am a Jew, from Tarsus in Cilicia, a citizen of no mean city."

We know only a little about Paul's home life, but a few facts are plain. He was born and reared in an orthodox Jewish family, where he was trained to obey all the Jewish laws. His family were Pharisees, a group of Jewish people who followed strict religious laws. In Jewish history the Pharisees are much like the Puritans in American history. A sturdy breed of strong character and determined courage, they often insisted on little rules and regulations. The Pharisees believed that they were more righteous and holy than ordinary men. They fasted more than others and wore austere clothing to show that they were men of God. Paul himself once said: "According to the strictest party of our religion I have lived as a Pharisee."

We know also that Paul's father was a Roman citizen. This was a special honor, and it probably means that Paul's family was well-to-do with a fairly influential standing in the synagogue and in the city. Roman citizenship was granted for various reasons—sometimes for outstanding service to the community, sometimes as a method of persuading colonists to settle in new areas, sometimes in return for money. There were special rights and privileges reserved for Roman citizens, and more than once Paul had reason to be grateful for them.

From the few facts we know we can picture Saul of Tarsus as a privileged and highly gifted boy, with a family that was very proud of him. A spiritually sensitive lad, he was trained at the synagogue school in the rich heritage of the Jewish people. And eventually he decided—at what age we do not know—to become a rabbi, a doctor or teacher of the law.

Paul's father must have rejoiced at that decision and decided that his son should have the best

education a rabbi could get. At any rate, Paul went to Jerusalem to study under the great teacher, Gamaliel. How old he was when he went to Jerusalem to study we do not know. Most probably he was in his later teens.

While still a youth Paul also learned a trade. Every Jewish rabbi was required to have a trade, so that he could earn his own living. This enabled the rabbis to teach the people in school and syna-gogue without being paid for it. Paul's trade was making cloth out of goat's hair. He must have started learning to do this while in Tarsus, for the cloth which he made took its name of "Cilicium" from the province of Cilicia, where Tarsus was located. Paul probably made the fabric and then worked it into sails for ships or into tents used by caravans and by the Roman armies.

Saul, or Paul, must have felt very fortunate as he settled down to his studies in Jerusalem. He was the son of a prosperous family, a serious young man dedicated to becoming a good rabbi. In addition, he was equipped with a trade so that he could support himself. But there was trouble ahead.

Shortly before Paul came to Jerusalem, Jesus had been crucified there on Calvary. Rumors about Jesus may have reached Paul in Tarsus, but so far as is known Paul never saw Jesus during the time of His ministry in Palestine. In Jerusalem, however, Paul ran headlong into the problems presented by Jesus' eager and devoted followers. At first these "believers" were not many in number. One hundred and twenty persons, we are told, were in the group at the beginning. But soon the numbers rose. Luke tells us that after Peter's sermon at Pentecost three thousand new disciples joined the group.

Paul was no doubt puzzled at first by these strange fanatics—for so they must have seemed to him. They believed that the glorious Messiah of the Jews, the redeemer whose coming had been foretold by the prophets, had already appeared in the person of the humble carpenter Jesus whom the Romans had crucified. But soon Paul was not only puzzled; he was provoked and angry. This crazy movement, he thought, was downright treachery against the Jewish faith, and it must be crushed.

The storm that was brewing in Jerusalem against the followers of Jesus soon broke out in violence, and its first victim was a man named Stephen. Unlike Peter, James, John and the rest of the twelve original disciples, Stephen was not a Jew who had been born and brought up in Palestine. Instead, he had lived somewhere in the Greek world. Such men were called "Hellenists." There were millions of them, faithful Jews, scattered all over the Roman Empire. In their synagogues the Scriptures were read in Greek, for many were unfamiliar with Aramaic, the language of the Jews of Palestine. Paul himself was a Hellenist. Though a loyal Jew, he spoke Greek in Tarsus and naturally shared many of his Greek friends' ways of thinking.

There was a natural difference between these Hellenists and the Jews who had lived all their lives in Palestine. The Hellenists often had a broader outlook; they had lived in the great world of their day and had shared its thought. Even in Jerusalem itself the Hellenists had a synagogue of their own where they no doubt felt more at home. Paul almost certainly attended that synagogue, where Greek was doubtless spoken. Very probably even the Old Testament was read in its famous Greek translation, which Paul in his letters frequently quotes.

Another attendant at that synagogue was certainly Stephen, whom Luke describes as "full of grace and power." Like many another Hellenist, Stephen had joined Jesus' followers, and had accepted Christ as his lord and savior. This, however, did not make Stephen think that he was no longer a Jew. Had not Jesus himself been a Jew all his life, even though he did disagree with the Pharisees? The first followers of Jesus still clung to the synagogues and to their Jewish loyalties and habits. But they argued in the synagogue, trying to persuade their fellow Jews that Jesus was the Messiah. Naturally this aroused angry opposition.

Stephen especially was a very forceful speaker. He attracted so much attention and stirred up so much antagonism that he was called before the Jewish supreme council to defend himself. On that fateful occasion he surely did not give in or compromise. And he ended by denouncing the orthodox Jews for the way in which they had always persecuted their forward-looking prophets and had now betrayed and murdered the Righteous One, Jesus. According to Luke's account, the members of the council "were enraged, and they ground their teeth against him."

That was a tragic day for Paul. He saw and heard the argument. And he shared the anger of the crowd that took Stephen out of the city and stoned him until he died. As a result of the cruel and

11

brutal thing they did, Stephen became the first Christian martyr. Now we would call it mob murder, but the Jewish leaders who superintended the killing did not think of it in that way. They had an ancient law, written down in *Deuteronomy*, one of the books of the Old Testament. And they thought it covered the case: "You shall stone him to death with stones, because he sought to draw you away from the Lord your God."

Paul not only witnessed the stoning—Luke says he "was consenting to his death"—he even helped.

Paul's Youth

He stood guard over the garments of the killers while they went about their deadly work. Whoever could have guessed that that young man, Saul of Tarsus, would in the end be a Christian martyr himself? But in reading Luke's account in *The Acts,* one feels sure that Paul's inward struggle started on the day he saw Stephen stoned. For as death drew near, Stephen prayed, "Lord Jesus, receive my spirit," and then he cried with a loud voice, "Lord, do not hold this sin against them."

How is it possible that Luke ever found out such intimate facts, which only an eyewitness could have known? It is quite likely that Paul told him, for Paul would never have been able to forget that scene.

II

Paul's Conversion

If ever a man destined to greatness in the history of the Christian church got off to a bad start it was Paul. As he wrote in his letter to the Galatians, "I persecuted the church of God violently and tried to destroy it." To be sure, he was not alone in this. The Jewish leaders felt just the way he did and supported him. They did not see themselves as bigots persecuting another religion; they saw themselves as faithful Jews, loyal to their great heritage. It was their duty to crush out these fanatics who were proclaiming a false Messiah. So, although Paul's behavior may seem dreadful to us now, he was acting with a clear conscience. Later on, according to Luke, when Paul was talking about his past life, he said:

> *I myself was convinced that I ought to do many things in opposing the name of Jesus of Nazareth. And I did so in Jerusalem; I not only shut up many of the saints in prison, by authority from the chief priests, but when they were put to death I cast my vote against them. And I punished them often in all the synagogues . . . and in raging fury against them I persecuted them even to foreign cities.*

It is plain that, if we are to understand Paul, we must try to understand the tremendous change that took place in him. What turned him from being this cruel persecutor of Jesus' followers into being Christ's great apostle? He talked afterward about being "transformed by the renewal of your mind," and certainly no one ever experienced a more complete transformation than he did. Picture him in those early days when, as Luke says, "Saul laid waste the church." Then picture him years later looking back with penitent shame on his persecutions, and writing: "I am the least of the apostles, unfit to be called an apostle, because I persecuted the church of God." What a complete change!

To begin with, of course, a man as intelligent as Paul could not possibly have oppressed the followers of Jesus as he did without learning what they believed and what kind of person their Lord and Master was. Paul himself says that he "tried to make them blaspheme." That is, he tried to persuade them to renounce Jesus, give up their faith in him, and forsake his cause. Sending Jesus' followers to prison and killing them was the last resort. What Paul would have liked best of all would have been to win them back to their old Jewish orthodoxy. So he must have argued with them and they with him. All the time, without his realizing it, Paul was being instructed in what those first disciples knew and believed about Jesus.

Moreover, he must have come in contact with

Paul's Conversion

some impressive characters—men and women of strong faith and courage who, like Stephen, lived admirably, declared their convictions persuasively, and died nobly. One suspects that there were occasions when Paul, against his own wish and will, felt half unconsciously that those followers of Jesus had something vital in their faith which gave them inner strength, courage, and hope. Paul was not simply persecuting the church. He himself was being exposed to what the church believed and knew about Jesus. And this was having a secret effect which Paul probably did not recognize. Or if he did he tried to brush it aside. Indeed, so strange are the workings of man's secret motives that Paul's increasing fury as he ravaged the church may well have been caused by a struggle going on within himself. Perhaps he attacked the followers of Jesus all the more violently because deep within he sometimes felt the goading temptation to become one of them.

Then came the climax!

One day Paul was traveling from Jerusalem to the city of Damascus. As Luke puts it, he was "breathing threats and murder against the disciples of the Lord." Suddenly, when he drew near Damascus, a light brighter than the sun shone on him and his company. It blinded him so that he fell to the ground. Then he heard a voice saying, "Saul, Saul, why do you persecute me?" And when the blinded man asked who was speaking to him, the voice answered, "I am Jesus, whom you are persecuting; but rise and enter the city and you will be told what you are to do."

In *The Acts of the Apostles* there are three accounts of Paul's experience on the Damascus Road. They differ in some details, but the major fact is clear in all of them. Paul, in a tremendous crisis of sudden enlightenment, was changed from a foe of Jesus to his devoted disciple and apostle. Of course this sudden, dramatic conversion was a serious shock, and Paul's blindness remained with him for three days.

However we may explain this experience, or even if we simply wonder what the explanation is, the important fact is clear. Saul of Tarsus, who had been ravaging the church, became Paul the

Paul's Conversion

Apostle. In one of the three accounts which Luke includes in his book, the voice says to Saul, "It hurts you to kick against the goads." A goad is a sharp-pointed stick used to drive oxen. Luke's figure of speech pictures what had been going on inside Saul. All his experiences with the followers of Jesus, his increasing insight into what Jesus said and did, the strong arguments of convinced believers in Jesus, their brave and radiant characters—all this had been goading him to be one with them, not against them. How he had kicked against that goad! But now the fight was over. He went into Damascus and joined the community of believers there.

One of the leading men among Jesus' followers in Damascus was named Ananias. At first Ananias was reluctant to go to Paul; he knew the dreadful things Paul had done to the church. But when he was convinced that a real change had taken place, he gave Paul a joyous welcome into the Christian fellowship, saying, "Saul, my brother, the Lord has sent me." So the new disciple was baptized and a new era began in the church's history.

At this point we come upon one of those places in Paul's life where we wish we had more exact information. In his letter to the Galatians, Paul wrote that after joining the Christian fellowship in Damascus he "went away into Arabia," and later "returned to Damascus." How the imagination of Christian scholars has played on that visit to Arabia! Where in Arabia? What did he do in Arabia?

A likely explanation would seem to be something like this. For Paul to become a believer in

Paul's Conversion

Jesus meant the upset and overturn of his whole way of thinking and living. He faced a serious re-arrangement of his life, and beyond that he faced the necessity of rethinking his basic ideas about religion. This could not be done in a day. He needed time. He wanted to get away from the crowd and readjust his mind to his new faith. Many scholars think he retreated to some quiet place in Arabia, on the very edge of which stood Damascus. There he thought through the meaning of this crucial experience which had befallen him. Then he returned to Damascus, prepared to proclaim the good news about Jesus with the same power and zest he had once used in speaking and acting against Him.

Naturally Paul began speaking in the synagogues. We know that there were then many thousands of Jews in Damascus. Even the followers of Jesus, while they doubtless had meetings of their own in their homes, still worshiped in the synagogues on the Sabbath.

If Paul expected a warm welcome from the Jews he certainly did not receive it. He was now saying the same kind of thing Stephen had been stoned for saying. And trained as he was to be a rabbi, Paul was probably saying it better. If Stephen deserved to be stoned, the Jews of Damascus must have thought, Why not Paul? His proclamation of Jesus as the Messiah was bad enough. What made it worse was the fact that Paul, lately a persecutor of Jesus' followers, had now joined them. He had become a deserter, a turncoat, a traitor. So the Jewish leaders turned in fury against Paul.

In one of his letters to the Corinthians Paul says that he was flogged by the Jews on five occasions—thirty-nine lashes each time. The law permitted flogging with forty lashes, but the habitual practice was to make it thirty-nine, just in case there might be a mistake in counting. We do not have in Paul's letters or in *The Acts of the Apostles* any record of these five floggings, but it is not unreasonable to suppose that the first one took place in Damascus. We do know that in the end the Damascus Jews decided to kill Paul. Perhaps they tried flogging him first and then, when that

Paul's Conversion

did not stop him, made up their minds to kill him. So Paul had to go into hiding.

Damascus was a walled city, with only a few gates by which one could enter or leave. All these gates the Jews guarded, and the leader of the Arabs in the city, doubtless persuaded that Paul was a dangerous man, conspired with them. They were determined to catch Paul if he tried to escape. Well, he did escape. One night his friends took him into a room in the city's outer wall. There they put him into a basket which they had prepared and lowered him by ropes from a window in the wall. Today Damascus has about a mile of its city wall still standing, and the tourist is shown a window out of which Paul is supposed to have made his dangerous escape. One does not need to believe that this is in truth the very window from which Paul was dropped in order to feel how exciting and perilous was the start of Paul's Christian ministry.

From Damascus Paul went to Jerusalem. The distance in a straight line is about a hundred and fifty miles, but it was longer as Paul walked the winding roads. He had been away from Jerusalem for three years while living in Damascus and Arabia. Now above all else he wanted to return to the Holy City—not, we may be sure, to see his old teacher, Gamaliel, but to see Simon Peter, the fisherman from Galilee, who could tell him about Jesus. Naturally Paul got a cold reception in Jerusalem. When last he was there, the priests and rabbis had been his admiring friends. Now they hated him as a deserter and a renegade. As for the followers of Jesus, they were suspicious of Paul. Luke tells us that "they were all afraid of him, for they did not believe that he was a disciple." No wonder! It was hard to accept as a loyal member of their fellowship a man who had so cruelly treated the Christians.

A disciple named Barnabas saved the day. The name means "Son of Encouragement," and Barnabas certainly was that to Paul. For he brought Paul before the suspicious followers of Jesus. Telling them about Paul's conversion and his fearless preaching in Damascus, Barnabas won a welcome for him.

Paul's Conversion

How did Barnabas alone feel so sure? We do not know. He was a Hellenist; he came from Cyprus, an island lying off the coast of Cilicia, south of Tarsus. Perhaps he had received first-hand news from Damascus about what had happened there. Anyway, he opened the door of welcome and confidence to the new disciple. Between the two men there began a long friendship and an influential partnership in Christian service.

Paul spent fifteen days in Jerusalem, mainly conferring with Simon Peter. Peter was a fisherman with little education; Paul had been trained in the best schools and under the leading teacher of Judaism. But for those two weeks we may be sure that Paul sat at the feet of Peter to learn from him. For Peter could tell him all about Jesus, what he said and did, and the details of his life and death and continued presence with his disciples. There were no written Gospels then, but Peter knew the whole story by heart. He had lived it with the Master himself, and no one can measure what those hours with Simon Peter meant to Paul.

Nevertheless, Paul himself was not content to be

altogether silent. He had formerly spoken in Jerusalem against Jesus; now he wanted Jerusalem to hear him speak for Jesus. But the Jewish leaders who had been his partners in his persecuting days could not endure this. Their plot to kill Paul grew fierce and dangerous. So, as Luke tells us: "When the brethren knew it, they brought him down to Caesarea, and sent him off to Tarsus." As Paul sailed up the coast toward his boyhood home, he must have wondered what kind of reception he would get there.

III

Paul at Antioch

Our information about Paul's life during the ten years following his return to Tarsus is very limited. How much we wish we knew what kind of welcome his family gave him. When last they had seen him, starting out to study under Gamaliel in Jerusalem, they had been so proud of him. And now, instead of becoming a learned rabbi, he had become one of the despised and persecuted followers of Jesus. That must have been a dreadful shock to a rigid Jewish Pharisee like Paul's father. Paul never mentions his father in his letters, but twice he warns fathers about the way not to treat children. In one place he writes, "Fathers, do not provoke your children to anger," and again, "Fathers, do not provoke your children, lest they became discouraged." Perhaps those warnings came out of Paul's own experience. Perhaps he was not even welcomed home at all, and instead lived alone and supported himself by his trade as a tentmaker. One suspects that those years were among the most disheartening he ever spent.

But he did not give in. He kept on preaching the good news about Jesus to everyone whom he could reach. He started with the synagogues, speaking to the Jews there, and also to the Gentiles who had been attracted by the Jewish faith in one God. A good many of these Gentiles had become disgusted with the belief in many gods—a god of the sea, of the sky, a goddess of the hunt, of love, and so on. They were acquainted with the best of Greek thought, which had undermined this old belief in many gods. When, therefore, they came in contact with Judaism and its strong emphasis on one God, Creator of the universe, Maker of our bodies, Father of our spirits, they were often attracted by that faith. In fact they were frequently persuaded to accept it. Sometimes they joined the synagogues, were circumcised, observed the Sabbath laws and the rules of clean and unclean foods, and became practicing Jews. More often they remained on the fringe of the synagogue, holding to the Jewish faith in one God and to the high ethics of the prophets. Apparently, more and more Paul found himself appealing successfully to these Gentiles with his message about Jesus.

At any rate the evidence seems clear that he went about the provinces of Cilicia and Syria, presenting his gospel so powerfully that Christian churches were founded in one town after another. A few years later, we read, "he went through Syria and Cilicia, strengthening the churches." And we know of no one who could have started the churches for which he cared so much except Paul himself.

Meanwhile important matters were afoot in the

city of Antioch, in northern Syria. It was one of the greatest cities in the Roman Empire. "Antioch, the Beautiful," "The Queen of the East"—by such names it was called. It had probably a million inhabitants, including a large Jewish population, and the synagogue there was, next to the one in Alexandria, the most magnificent in the world. Josephus, the Jewish historian, a contemporary of Paul's, said that a very large number of Gentile converts were associated with this synagogue. So when the followers of Jesus began speaking to the people of the synagogue they found themselves dealing not only with Jews from Palestine and Hellenistic Jews from the Greek world, but also with Gentiles who never had been Jews. The towering question, therefore, was inevitable: *In order to become a Christian did a Gentile have first to become a Jew? Did he have to be circumcised, and then must he observe all the little rules about Sabbath keeping and kosher food?*

To us, whether we are Christians or Jews, that question now seems utterly unreal, but it was very urgent in the church of Paul's time. There was a

Paul at Antioch

powerful party among the followers of Jesus which insisted that any Gentile joining the Christian fellowship must first become a Jew and comply with all the Jewish laws. If that party had gained control, Christianity would have been, not one of the world's great religions, but only a Jewish sect. Thus any Gentile wishing to become a Christian would be compelled first to become a Jew. That party, however, did not gain control, and the most outstanding personality who helped in the battle against it was Paul. In fact his most cherished title was "Apostle to the Gentiles."

In trying to understand the problem, we must remember that the disciples of Jesus were first called "Christians" in Antioch. In this book we have already used the word to describe the followers of Jesus, but the fact is they never had been called that until the people of Antioch began using the term "Christian"—perhaps as a nickname for them. Until then the followers of Jesus had simply been Jews who believed in him as the Messiah; they had had no separate and distinctive name. But now in Antioch they began to stand out as a distinct group and to attract attention. So it was natural that the question should rise: How does one join that group? What does it stand for? What are the conditions of membership in it?

Then something happened to make this question very urgent. According to Luke, the first disciple of Jesus who came to Antioch from Jerusalem spoke the good news about Jesus to nobody except Jews. But then others came—Hellenists from Cyprus and Cyrene—who spoke to the Greeks. That is, they spoke to Gentiles who never had been Jews. The effect was astonishing. A surprising number of the Gentiles welcomed the message about Jesus and, as Luke says, "a great number that believed turned to the Lord." Moreover, the church in Antioch broke away from the old restrictions and welcomed the Gentile converts, baptizing them at once into the Christian fellowship.

All of this was certainly disturbing news to many of the conservative members of the Jerusalem church. They had never even entered the house of a Gentile or eaten at the same table with one. So the Jerusalem church sent a representative

Paul at Antioch

to Antioch to see what was going on. Fortunately the man they chose was Paul's friend, Barnabas. He was, as Luke says, "a good man, full of the Holy Spirit and of faith." And Barnabas was delighted with the way the Gentiles in Antioch were being reached by the gospel and added to the church. He encouraged the liberal attitude which the Christians of Antioch had taken, and we may be sure he sent back an encouraging report to the still reluctant Jewish church members in Jerusalem.

Then Barnabas did something which was to have tremendous historic consequences. Though it had been about a decade since he had last seen Paul, Barnabas must have had news of him preaching in Tarsus and its neighboring towns and cities, founding new churches, and having outstanding success in winning the attention and achieving the conversion of Gentiles. What the church in Antioch was doing for the Gentiles there, Paul was doing elsewhere. Thus he was just the man Barnabas needed to help him. So Barnabas traveled the eighty miles from Antioch to Tarsus, persuaded Paul to join him, and together they went to

Antioch and became teammates in one of the most important movements in the early church. Luke at first called the team "Barnabas and Saul," but before long he changed the sequence to "Paul and Barnabas."

Happy and fortunate though they were in their work in Antioch, Paul and Barnabas were constantly troubled by their old-fashioned brethren in the Jerusalem church. These leaders insisted that no Gentile could enter the Christian fellowship without first becoming a Jew. To be sure, even the Jerusalem church was not unanimous on that point. Peter, for example, had an experience which at first shocked many. While troubled by this question about welcoming Gentiles into the Christian fellowship, he had a dream in which he saw a great sheet let down from the sky by its four corners. It contained "all kinds of animals and reptiles and birds of the air." A voice said to him: "Rise, Peter, kill and eat." But Peter in his dream protested against that. All his old devotion to the laws of kosher food rose in revolt. "No Lord," he said, "for I have never eaten anything that is common or un-

clean." Then the voice spoke to him a second time: "What God has cleansed, you must not call common." Of course Jesus had said the same thing. He had brushed aside the laws of kosher food. But even so Peter found it hard to break with his old ideas and habits.

Then while he was "inwardly perplexed," messengers came to him from Cornelius, a Roman centurion, asking Peter to come and see him. Cornelius, of course, was a Gentile, "an upright and God-fearing man" who had been deeply influenced by the Jewish faith. But he was still an uncircumcised Gentile. Under the influence of his dream, however, Peter went to Cornelius' house, and an extraordinary result followed. Peter welcomed the desire expressed by Cornelius to hear about Jesus, and he poured out his heart in telling the company gathered in Cornelius' home the story of the Master's life and teaching. They all were deeply moved. Luke says that "the Holy Spirit fell on all who heard the word." They accepted the new faith and were baptized. Peter even said: "I perceive that God knows no partiality, but in every nation any one who fears him and does what is right is acceptable to him." The conservative church members in Jerusalem, however, did not like Peter's liberality. "Why did you go to uncircumcised men," they cried, "and eat with them?" That was all the response their narrow-mindedness could think of.

Such prejudiced people were to be one of Paul's chief problems all his life, and part of his solution was to try to be good to them. For example, during that first year when Barnabas and Paul were working together in Antioch, the fear of a coming famine grew more and more disturbing. The rains were failing; drought was threatening the crops. One messenger from Jerusalem, Agabus by name, came to Antioch predicting that a widespread famine was on its way. At once the Christians in Antioch seized on this situation as a way of expressing, despite all differences of opinion, their abiding and loyal good will to their Jerusalem brethren. They gathered gifts of money—"everyone according to his ability," says Luke—and Barnabas and Paul were elected to carry this relief to Jerusalem.

Paul at Antioch

To be sure, some Christians in the Holy City might not agree with all that the two men from Antioch were doing, but when such generous, unasked-for help came in the hands of Barnabas and Paul, they must have felt the genuine Christian spirit of the church in Antioch.

Though this trip of Barnabas and Paul to Jerusalem brought relief to the physical need of the church there, it had another far-reaching and important result. When Barnabas returned to Antioch with Paul, he brought with him his young cousin, John Mark. What an amazing man Barnabas was! As we shall see later, we have reason to believe that he was a very impressive-looking person, and his wisdom and courage are evident. But the greatest service he rendered was his discovery of two men who were even greater than he. If it had not been for Barnabas, Paul might have spent the rest of his life in Tarsus. It was Barnabas who opened before him the doors of world-wide opportunity. And it was Barnabas who discovered John Mark, and put him to work.

Mark's mother, Mary, was one of the first

Christians in Jerusalem, and her home was one of the main centers where the early disciples gathered. One night, for example, Peter escaped from the prison where his enemies had put him. Before he fled the city he wanted to let the other disciples know that he had escaped. Where would he find them? He headed straight for the home of John Mark's mother and found the disciples there praying for him. They were exultant when he appeared.

Mark certainly fulfilled the hopes of the wonderful mother who had raised him. For first he was a close companion of Paul and, despite one misunderstanding between them, remained a devoted friend to the end. Even more important, Mark became the close associate of Peter. In fact he was his interpreter, for Peter could not speak Greek. And, finally, Mark was to be the author of the Gospel now known by his name, the earliest of the four Gospels in the New Testament. Here Mark wrote out for all the world the memories of Jesus which Peter had transmitted to him. In discovering Mark, Barnabas again proved that he was one of those remarkable men who see the possibilities in other people and help to bring them out to the best advantage.

Thus the work in Antioch flourished, and the missionary spirit grew. The leaders of the church felt strongly that the whole world must hear the gospel of Jesus. And in the end they gave a special commission to Barnabas and Paul. One day the two apostles, along with John Mark, sailed out of the harbor of Seleucia, headed for Cyprus.

IV

An Exciting Journey

Cyprus is the third largest island in the Mediterranean Sea. Look at the map on pages 54–55 and you will see it lying southwest of the harbor of Seleucia. In Paul's day Cyprus was well known for its copper mines. Although the island was mainly populated by Greeks, Jews were there also. Since Barnabas had at one time lived on Cyprus, the apostles may well have had friends and family to welcome them when the ship landed at Salamis. Starting at Salamis

46

An Exciting Journey

Paul, Barnabas, and Mark traveled over the one-hundred-mile length of the island to Paphos, its capital city, telling the story of Jesus in the synagogues. When the Jews rejected them, Paul and Barnabas turned to the Gentiles with their message. They attracted so much attention that at last Sergius Paulus, the Roman proconsul in Paphos, invited them to call on him.

Like many ancient officials, this Roman proconsul had on his staff a magician or astrologer who was supposed to have secret powers. It was said he could foresee what was going to happen, and very probably he also claimed to know cures for various sicknesses. He was present while Paul addressed the proconsul, and he saw that Paul was evidently making a strong impression on Sergius Paulus.

Who are these fellows? he doubtless thought. Are they another kind of magician who will displace me? He interrupted Paul and tried to silence him. We call Paul a saint, but he had a temper and on occasion it could flare up hotly. He turned on the magician and said: "You son of the devil, you

enemy of all righteousness, full of all deceit and villainy, will you not stop making crooked the straight paths of the Lord?" The magician collapsed. Perhaps he had a brain spasm; in any case he went temporarily blind. The proconsul was greatly impressed. He thought it was a miracle, and Luke says that he "believed, when he saw what had occurred."

This is the first encounter we know of between Paul and a Roman official. Many more were to follow, but this was the beginning. Perhaps that is

An Exciting Journey

the reason why Luke at this point in *The Acts of the Apostles* starts using the name "Paul." Until this incident at Paphos he has referred to the Apostle by his Hebrew name, Saul. Now he begins using the Roman name, Paul, and the missionary team becomes "Paul and his company" or "Paul and Barnabas."

When they sailed away from Cyprus, their ship headed north and landed them at Perga, in the province of Pamphylia. Probably they intended to carry on their missionary work there, but something happened to prevent it. The most probable explanation is that Paul became ill. We know that he did suffer from an illness which he called "a thorn in the flesh," and from which he prayed in vain to be delivered. Many guesses have been made as to what this illness was, but malaria seems a very likely choice. It is easy to think of Paul smitten with malarial fever at Perga, on the marshy seacoast of Asia Minor, where the mosquitoes that cause malaria thrive. Of course no one then knew the cause or the cure for this sickness. Apparently, though, they had discovered that if the sick man left the marshy seacoast and climbed to the highlands he grew better. So Paul and Barnabas changed their plans and climbed the hills to Pisidian Antioch—not the Antioch in Syria mentioned earlier. Pisidian Antioch was about four thousand feet above sea level, and apparently Paul regained his strength while he was there.

Meanwhile Mark had left them and gone back to Jerusalem. Paul did not like this at all. It seemed to him that Mark was quitting. So when Paul reached the highlands a hundred miles from Perga, he was both a sick and disappointed man. If, however, we suppose that he was a defeated man we do not know Paul. He turned that discouraging situation into one of the most useful victories of his life. For while there he founded the churches of Galatia. Years afterward he wrote to the Galatians: "You know it was because of a bodily ailment that I preached the gospel to you at first; and though my condition was a trial to you, you did not scorn or despise me, but received me as an angel of God."

Apparently, then, some aftereffects of the ma-

An Exciting Journey

laria still plagued Paul in the highlands. But judging by his strenuous living and his undaunted courage, his health must have improved decidedly. He spoke in the synagogue of Pisidian Antioch on the Sabbath, tracing the history of Israel until its consummation in the coming of Jesus Christ. The people were so impressed that they begged Paul to speak more the following Sabbath. We are told by Luke that "many Jews and devout converts to Judaism" sought Paul out and listened receptively to his instruction. On the next Sabbath a great crowd filled the synagogue and Paul spoke again. This time, however, the unbelieving Jews contradicted him and made further speaking in the synagogue impossible. So Paul and Barnabas said they would turn to the Gentiles. And that they did with such success their enemies stirred up a bitter conspiracy against them and forced them to leave the city.

We must try sympathetically to understand those Jews who feared and persecuted Paul. This new message about Jesus' being their Messiah was very disturbing to them. Their Messiah crucified! They were shocked by the idea. Moreover they began to see that these new Christians were not going to remain just another Jewish sect, like the Pharisees, the Sadducees, or the Essenes. The Jewish elders were used to differing parties inside Judaism, and they could have stood that. But these Christians were going to be a separate group, a new kind of religion with churches of their own. Along with their many Gentile converts, they were going to take to themselves some of the most valuable members of the synagogues. Since these Jewish elders were right in foreseeing that Paul and his companions were blazing the trail for a new religion, it is no wonder that they were "filled with jealousy," as Luke says.

After Paul and Barnabas were forced to leave Pisidian Antioch, they walked the eighty or more miles to the Galatian town Iconium. Here once more they spoke in the synagogue. And once again they had their familiar experience of finding their message welcomed, as Luke puts it, by "a great company . . . both of Jews and of Greeks." But, as before, they soon faced the growing hatred of the

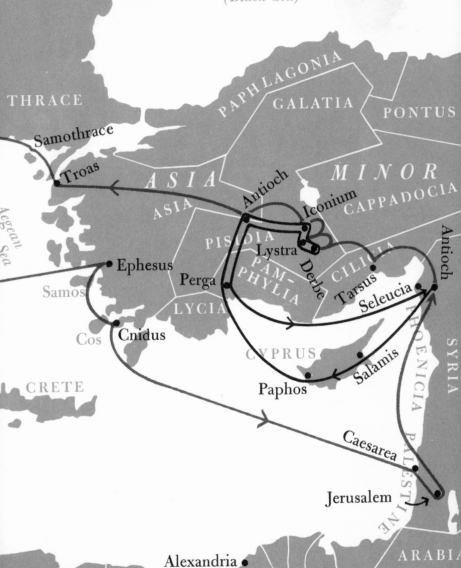

PONTUS EUXIMUS
(Black Sea)

THRACE

Samothrace

Troas

Aegean Sea

Ephesus

Samos

Cos

Cnidus

CRETE

PAPHLAGONIA

GALATIA

PONTUS

ASIA

MINOR

CAPPADOCIA

ASIA

Antioch

Iconium

PISIDIA

Lystra

Derbe

CILICIA

Antioch

Perga

PAM-
PHYLIA

Tarsus

Seleucia

LYCIA

PHOENICIA

CYPRUS

SYRIA

Salamis

Paphos

Caesarea

PALESTINE

Jerusalem

ARABIA

Alexandria

EGYPT

An Exciting Journey

unbelieving Jews until at last they were threatened with being stoned to death. So they left Iconium and after a six-hour journey reached the town of Lystra. Here they found no synagogue at all and their appeal was made directly to the Gentiles.

The exciting and nearly fatal events which befell them at Lystra began with Paul's healing of a crippled man. We are not told the exact nature of his handicap, but he was evidently a cripple well known to his fellow townsmen. And he was listening to Paul preach. Paul became interested in the man, made his acquaintance, saw in him a spark of faith which could be fanned into a blaze, and at last said to him, "Stand upright on your feet." This the man did, and the news roused the whole town. "A miracle!" they all said. And then they cried, "The gods have come down to us in the likeness of men." Barnabas was the more impressive looking of the two men, so the townspeople started to call him Zeus, the name of the greatest of the Greek gods. Paul, who did most of the talking, they called Hermes, after the herald and messenger of the Greek gods. This now seems incredible, but the people of Lystra still believed quite literally in the old mythology. Only with difficulty did Barnabas and Paul prevent the local priest of Zeus from offering animals in sacrifice to them.

So the two apostles got a good hearing in Lystra, and a Christian group was formed. As far as we know it was made up mostly, if not altogther, of Gentiles. But trouble was brewing back in Pisidian Antioch and Iconium from which the apostles lately had come. The orthodox Jews in those two cities were so incensed against Paul, so convinced that he was a real danger to all loyal Jews, that they determined to stone him to death. A crowd of them followed him all the way to Lystra. Catching him there in some unprotected moment, they stoned him and "dragged him out of the city, supposing that he was dead." That might easily have been the end of Paul. When his friends found him, he was still unconscious. Soon, however, they saw signs of life, and finally he was able to rise and enter the city, badly beaten and bruised but not killed.

Cruel though his experience at Lystra was, Paul had some happy memories of his ministry there, memories which lasted all his life. It was in Lystra, for example, that Paul found a young man named Timothy, who became one of his most valued and trusted companions. "Timothy, my beloved child," Paul calls him, and in passage after passage the references to this young disciple are grateful and affectionate. His mother was a Christian Jewess, his father a Greek. Paul, we may be sure, would have thought it worth-while being stoned if in the town where he was stoned he could find a faithful helper like Timothy.

After the stoning, however, they left Lystra for the town of Derbe, forty miles away. There they preached, made converts, and founded a church. In Derbe they also made a decision which reveals them as the brave and dauntless men they were. Ever since they had left Pisidian Antioch they had been traveling in the direction of Antioch in Syria, their home base, to which they intended to return. How easy it would have been to have kept on their homeward way. That would have been the natural and least demanding thing to do. But apparently Paul and Barnabas did not seriously consider doing it. They had on their hearts a burden of care for the churches they had founded. To be sure, Lystra, Iconium, and Pisidian Antioch were dangerous; the apostles had faced determined enemies there and might face them again. But back they went, retracing their steps through the perilous towns. They restored confidence in the Christian converts who had been shaken by the news of Paul's stoning. The apostles' faith and courage were contagious, and the new Christians responded to them with all the more assured reliance and trust. They organized the churches, appointed elders, and left behind them vital and growing groups which Paul would care for all his life with special affection. How Paul and Barnabas managed to avoid stirring up their old enemies we do not know, but probably they stayed away from the synagogues and worked quietly among the Christians.

In the end they finished their ministry in Pisidian Antioch and went down the hundred-mile slope to Perga on the seacoast, where they had landed when they came from Cyprus. At that time Paul's illness had prevented him from preaching there, but now he spoke in the synagogue. Afterward they took ship and sailed down the coast to their own home church in Syrian Antioch. What a home-coming that must have been! They had been away for perhaps three years. They had traveled about fourteen hundred miles, half by sea and half on land. Considering that the fastest transportation for them on the sea was a sailing ship and on land a donkey, their journey was surely an achievement. When they returned, Luke tells us, "they gathered the church together and declared all that God had done with them, and how he had opened a door of faith to the Gentiles." That was Paul's consuming passion now—to bring Christianity to the Gentiles.

Back in Pisidian Antioch, when Paul turned away from the unbelieving Jews who had rejected him, he had quoted to them a verse from the prophet Isaiah, where God says:

I have set you to be a light for the Gentiles,
That you may bring salvation to the uttermost
parts of the earth.

That was Paul's commission as he understood it, and it led him into one of the most adventurous and dangerous lives ever lived.

Indeed, although coming back to his home base in Antioch must have brought him deep satisfaction, it did not mean that all was joy and peace. There was trouble in the church in Antioch, serious trouble which threatened everything that Paul cared for most in his Gentile ministry. And immediately he was plunged into dealing with that disturbing situation.

V

A Well-fought Fight

The trouble in the church at Antioch was caused by some Jewish disciples from Jerusalem. These followers of Jesus came to Antioch, where they were badly upset about the way Jews and Gentiles together were coming into the church without any regard for the old Jewish laws. This would never do, they thought. To be a good Christian one must first become a good Jew and keep the laws of Moses concerning clean and unclean foods, behavior on the Sabbath, and all the rest. They thought this strongly and sincerely, and they said it forthrightly to the church members in Antioch.

We can imagine Paul's reaction. He was indignant. These good men from Jerusalem might be sincere, but he was sure that they were wrong. What saved a man and made a Christian of him was not rituals and rules. It was faith in Christ, inner power from Christ, and what Paul called "the fruit of the Spirit"—namely "love, joy, peace, patience, kindness, goodness, faithfulness, gentleness, self-control." This way of living was genuine Christianity, Paul thought. Circumcision and kosher food had nothing to do with it. If a Jew, when he became a Christian, wanted to keep on observing the old rules to which he had been accustomed, that was all right with Paul. But to tell a Gentile that he had to take on the burden of all the Mosaic rules before he could become a Christian was all wrong. And for Jewish Christians to refuse to eat with Gentile Christians, because they always had practiced that kind of segregation with non-Jews, was a deadly evil which would split up the church. Something had to be done about this. When Paul and Barnabas could get nowhere with the visitors from Jerusalem, they decided to go themselves to the apostles in Jerusalem and settle the matter. With the backing the church, a party headed by Paul and Barnabas went to Jerusalem. They took with them not only the arguments in their heads but an example of what they were fighting for—Titus, a young Greek who never had submitted himself to any Jewish ritual, but who was a vital, radiant Christian. Years later Paul called Titus "my true child in a common faith." So there may be truth in the old tradition that Paul found Titus in Iconium on his first missionary journey there and converted him to the Christian faith. Certainly Titus must have been an outstanding character if Paul and Barnabas took him to Jerusalem to show to Peter, James, and John as an example of how thoroughly Christian a Gentile could be, quite apart from the rituals and laws of ancient Judaism.

As was to be expected, Paul and Barnabas found that the church in Jerusalem was divided in

A Well-fought Fight

opinion about the important problem they had come to discuss. The outstanding leaders of the church, however—Peter, James, and John—received the embassy from Antioch with fraternal good will and gave their blessing to the work which Paul and Barnabas were doing among the Gentiles. They welcomed Titus also and did not require him to be circumcised. As Paul wrote later to the Galatians, the three leading apostles of the Jerusalem church "gave to me and Barnabas the right hand of fellowship, that we should go to the Gentiles."

This was a real victory. Many influences were behind this liberal stand by the apostles in Jerusalem. There were the great Hebrew prophets with their care for all mankind, not to mention the attitude of Jesus rebuking those who, obsessed with little rules and rituals, "tithe mint and rue and every herb, and neglect justice and the love of God." In addition, there were the living examples of men like Titus who had come into a vital Christian faith without traveling the road of Jewish ceremonies. Such influences played strongly on the larger-minded leaders of the Jerusalem church who set Paul free to go to the Gentiles. As he later wrote to the Galatians, "In Christ Jesus neither circumcision nor uncircumcision is of any avail, but faith working through love."

While the larger-minded leaders of the Jerusalem church took this liberal attitude, there was a minority group who were vehemently against it. Not only did they themselves cling to all the Pharisaic rules they had been trained to observe, but they insisted that no Gentile could ever become a Christian without submitting to the same regulations. Despite Titus and all the other admirable Gentile Christians, despite Paul and Barnabas and the thriving churches they were building with Greek converts, this narrow-minded party in Jerusalem kept insisting that it was necessary for these Gentiles "to keep the law of Moses."

Thus the conference in Jerusalem was a stormy one at times. Paul describes the narrow-minded party in blistering terms. "False brethren," he calls them, "secretly brought in, who slipped in to spy out our freedom which we have in Christ Jesus,

that they might bring us into bondage." One can imagine hot words flying in that conference, as Paul stood his ground, refusing to compromise. And eventually he returned to Antioch with the blessing of the apostles. Doubtless he was grateful for that.

A little later Peter visited Antioch and entered happily into the fellowship of the largely Gentile church there. But the trouble was not over yet. The group of "false brethren" in Jerusalem were still making trouble. As a result James, the head of the Christian church in Jerusalem, tried a compromise which he hoped would satisfy both parties. He wrote a letter welcoming Greek converts but demanding that they must avoid eating food which had been sacrificed to idols. It also required that they eat no meat of animals slain in ways the Jewish laws disapproved and that they not marry near relatives according to the definition of Jewish regulations.

At first these conditions did not seem too serious, and Luke's account pictures the church in Antioch as pleased with the compromise. But it was a dangerous arrangement. Enforced literally these rules meant that Jewish Christians had to be very careful about eating with Gentile Christians if they had any reason to suspect that the Gentiles had not observed the regulations about the way animals should be slain. In one of Shakespeare's plays, he makes a Jew say to a Christian: "I will buy with you, sell with you, talk with you, walk with you, and so following; but I will not eat with you, drink with you, nor pray with you." This was the required attitude of strictly orthodox Jews, and one can see why even a mild form of this attitude would disrupt a Christian church. Indeed, even Peter stopped eating with his Gentile brethren in Antioch, and Barnabas himself wavered.

Paul never mentions this letter of James's, but in one of his own letters to the Galatians he does say that he opposed Peter to his face. Judging by the future developments in the Antioch church, Paul won, and the compromising letter of James was apparently not taken very seriously. To use more modern terms, the minority party in Jerusalem was fighting for segregation in the church,

A Well-fought Fight

with uncircumcised Gentiles regarded as second-class members. But Paul was fighting for complete integration, with Jews and Gentiles enjoying equality.

Evidently the storm in Antioch calmed down, and one day Paul suggested to Barnabas that they make another journey to see how the churches they had founded were getting on. Barnabas agreed, but he wanted to take Mark with him. Paul would not consent to that. He still held it against Mark that the young man had returned home instead of finishing the previous missionary journey with them. Luke says that "there arose a sharp contention" between Paul and Barnabas. Neither of them would give in. Barnabas still had faith in Mark, saw great possibilities in him, and was determined to stand by him. As the years passed by, Paul came around to feel as Barnabas did about Mark. And one is glad to observe that years afterward, when Paul was writing to the Colossians, Mark was with him as a valued companion. In that letter Paul writes that Mark joins him in greeting. But at the time Paul started out on his second journey, he was still in doubt about him. So Barnabas took Mark and went to Cyprus, while Paul chose as his companion a Christian named Silas and started north to visit the churches in Galatia.

Silas was a member of the Jerusalem church, a Jewish Christian who evidently shared Paul's views about integrating the Jews and Gentiles in the Christian fellowship. Luke always calls him by his Hebrew name, Silas, but Paul always uses his Latin name, Silvanus. They made a powerful team, and their companionship was long and fruitful. One imagines them starting north from Antioch, little guessing what an unforgettable adventure they were going to face. Tarsus, Derbe, Lystra, Iconium, and on to Pisidian Antioch—so their journey ran. And the churches were doubtless strengthened and encouraged by their visit. One of the most important events in the early part of their journey was Paul's reunion with young Timothy at Lystra. Perhaps Paul missed Mark and wanted a young man like him as a traveling companion. At any rate he asked Timothy to go with him, and the choice proved to be a happy one.

Eventually Paul, Silas, and Timothy came to the end of the Christian domain. There were no more churches to visit farther north. But Paul, a daring adventurer as well as a man of God, was determined now to conquer new territory for Christ. For reasons which we do not fully know he found his first plans blocked. He wanted to go north into the province of Asia but he was stopped, probably by some untoward circumstance, and by an inward voice that discouraged the venture. Then he very much wanted to go into the province of Bithynia, but again he was stopped. So, thwarted in his first plans, he traveled westward until he came to Troas, a seaport on the northwest corner of what is now called Asia Minor.

One wonders what Paul's feelings were when he landed at Troas. He had traveled hundreds of miles from Pisidian Antioch without doing anything that Luke was later to think worth recording. No synagogues visited, no one converted to Christ, all his plans blocked—this must have been a disheartening experience. Paul could scarcely have guessed that his coming to Troas was one of the most fortunate things that ever happened to him, a prelude to one of the most important events in Christian history.

It was in Troas that Paul met Luke. We know this because throughout *The Acts,* until the tenth verse of the sixteenth chapter, Luke uses the third person—he and they—when writing of Paul and his companions. But suddenly, when Paul reaches Troas, Luke changes to the first person. He writes, "*We* sought to go into Macedonia, concluding that God had called *us* to preach the gospel to them."

How we wish we knew the full story of that meeting! It takes some guessing to put the facts together, but it is quite possible that something like this may have happened. We know that Luke was a Greek, and a physician. Paul calls him "Luke, the beloved physician." Picture Paul, then, coming down from the highlands to the coast and falling ill, perhaps with his old enemy malaria. Needing a physician he inquires about one and Luke is recommended to him. So the two men meet and are mutually attracted to each other. Luke helps Paul with his illness, and Paul introduces Luke to Christ so that Luke becomes a convert.

Then Luke did something which Christians in the western world should never forget. He persuaded Paul to carry the news about Christ across the Aegean Sea to Europe. Luke himself had come from Europe; his hometown was almost certainly Philippi in Macedonia. Now that he was a Christian himself, he wanted his fellow Macedonians to hear the gospel from the lips of Paul. *The Acts* tells the story in a way that modestly hides Luke's share in it. Paul had a vision in the night, we read, in which "a man of Macedonia was standing beseeching him and saying, 'Come over to Macedonia and help us.'" But how could Paul recognize a man in his dream as coming from Macedonia? All the evidence indicates that the Macedonians had no distinguishing oddities of dress. No, it is much more likely that Luke was the man from Macedonia. He beseeched Paul to cross the Aegean Sea and help his fellow countrymen. At last his persuasion prevailed, and one night Paul had a vision that confirmed his decision to carry the gospel to Europe. This was the reason, he must have thought, why his early plans had been blocked and he had come to Troas. God had had a purpose in mind beyond Paul's power to see. So Paul, Silas, Timothy, and Luke set sail. As Luke wrote, "We made a direct voyage to Samothrace."

VI

Paul Invades Europe

Samothrace, where Paul's ship stopped first, is an island in the Aegean Sea. It was famous then and is remembered still as the original location of the magnificent statue of Victory, which today is one of the chief art treasures of the Louvre Museum in Paris.

From Samothrace the four travelers sailed to Macedonia. There they went ten miles inland to Philippi, a large and thriving city where quite probably they lodged at first with Luke's family or friends. No synagogue existed in Philippi, but outside the city on the bank of a river there was a gathering place where on the Sabbath some Jewish women met to pray. Paul started his European mission there, and its first result was the conversion of Lydia, a successful business woman. (Luke calls her "a seller of purple goods who was a worshiper of God.") She accepted the gospel which Paul preached, and was baptized—the first woman in Europe to join the Christian fellowship.

Lydia evidently had an ample home, for she invited Paul and his companions to make their headquarters in her house. They lodged with her and, as more converts were added to the church in Philippi, the Sabbath services of worship were held under her roof. We know that Paul's mission flourished there for of all the churches he founded none was more loyal to him and more loved by him. Read Paul's letter to the Philippians in the New Testament, and you can feel the warmth of his gratitude for the church which began in Lydia's home. "I thank my God," he writes to them, "in all my remembrance of you, always in every prayer of mine for you all and making my prayer with joy, thankful for your partnership in the gospel from the first day until now."

Even in Philippi, however, Paul ran into trouble. It started with a slave girl who was a ventriloquist. Today we use ventriloquism for entertainment, but the ancient world had another idea of it altogether. A ventriloquist speaks as though someone else were speaking through him, and the people of Paul's time thought that superhuman spirits or demons were actually using the vocal chords of the ventriloquist to bring a message from the unseen world. So this slave girl was very valuable to her owners. When she told fortunes or made predictions in a voice that was plainly not her own, people paid money to get the messages. For they supposed that the words came from spirits and demons. Because the people thought that she had this gift, probably the slave girl herself thought she had it. Then one day she heard Paul and his companions speak and was deeply impressed. "These men are servants of the Most

81

High God," she cried, "who proclaim the way of salvation."

Unfortunately the slave girl kept on crying this. She followed Paul around whenever she had the chance, shouting that he and his companions were men of God. "This she did for many days," Luke tells us, until Paul could stand it no longer. Turning sternly on her, he said to the spirit which he thought was using her, "I charge you in the name of Jesus Christ to come out of her."

The result was disastrous. The slave girl collapsed and refused to use her gift any more. Her owners were enraged at thus losing their source of income. They seized Paul and Silas, dragged them into the market place, and brought them before the magistrates. There they cried: "These men are Jews and they are disturbing our city. They advocate customs which it is not lawful for us Romans to accept or practice." This stirred up the crowd, who attacked Paul and his companion. The angry magistrates ordered the Christians to be flogged. Then the jailer "put them into the inner prison and fastened their feet in the stocks."

Impossible as it may seem, that was one of the greatest nights in Paul's experience. Although beaten and wounded, he and Silas recovered their high spirits, and at midnight they had all the other prisoners listening to them in amazement as they prayed and sang hymns. Then an earthquake struck Philippi, a not unusual happening in that area. But this time the tremor was severe enough to shake open the prison doors and loosen the stocks.

The jailer awoke, badly frightened because he expected the prisoners to run away. He was ready to kill himself rather than face the disgrace their escape would bring down on him. When Paul called out that the prisoners were all there, the jailer was so grateful that he listened with open mind and heart to Paul and Silas. At last he cried, "Men, what must I do to be saved?" They told him to believe in Jesus Christ, and before the night was over he and his family were baptized as Christians. Instead of being a jailer to Paul and Silas, he became a most hospitable host, bathing their wounds, welcoming them to his home, and setting food before them.

In the morning the magistrates sent policemen to the jail with orders to let the two men go free. But Paul was not willing to let the magistrates get off so easily. He and Silas were representatives of the Christian cause, and they had done nothing to deserve the mistreatment they had received. They were not going to leave behind them in Philippi a bad public record of a jail sentence. So Paul said: "They have beaten us publicly, uncondemned, men who are Roman citizens, and have thrown us into prison; and do they now cast us out secretly? No! Let them come themselves and take us out." When the police reported Paul's words, the magistrates were frightened. To flog a Roman citizen who had not been convicted of a crime was a serious offense. It was the magistrates, not Paul and Silas, who were now in trouble. They went to the jail and apologized for their conduct. And in order to prevent further difficulty they asked Paul and Silas to leave the city.

Put Paul in the worst imaginable situation, and he always succeeded in making the best of it. In his letter to the Philippians he wrote a sentence which has been happily translated: "Through him who strengthens me I am able for anything." When he wrote that, he could well have been thinking of the night he spent in the jail in Philippi.

So Paul, Silas, and Timothy left Philippi. But Luke remained behind to help guide the newly formed church. The others, meanwhile, traveled nearly ninety miles westward to Thessalonica, the provincial capital of Macedonia. There in the synagogue Paul had an exciting experience. His message caught fire and was welcomed both by Jews and by "a great many of the devout Greeks and not a few of the leading women." His stay in Thessalonica could not have been more than six months, but he founded a church there which endured and had a far-flung influence. As he later wrote to the Thessalonians, "You are our glory and joy."

Even Paul's successful experience at Thessalonica, however, brought trouble with it. Some influential Jews were disturbed by the conversion of their fellow Jews and Greek proselytes to faith in Jesus Christ. They gathered a rabble and set out to seize Paul at the house of Jason, a prominent Christian citizen whose home was Paul's headquarters. The mob did not find Paul and Silas, but they dragged Jason before the city authorities. There they accused the Christians of treason against the Roman emperor for asserting that "there is another king, Jesus."

The city authorities were greatly disturbed, but Jason was a well-known citizen. When he gave security that the troublesome visitors would leave the city, they let him go. So once more Paul and Silas found themselves unwelcome guests and slipped away by night to Beroea, a city fifty miles west of Thessalonica.

Beroea was the most populous city in Macedonia, and with undaunted vigor Paul started preaching the gospel of Jesus Christ in the synagogue there. Once more he received a warm welcome from certain of the Jews and from not a few of the better educated Greek men and women. But this peaceful and encouraging reception did not last long. News of Paul's success in Beroea got back to Thessalonica, and his Jewish enemies there came to Beroea. These enemies incited the crowds to such dangerous hatred that a group of Christians took Paul from the city down to the seaport. Finding a ship about to sail, they accompanied Paul on the nearly two-hundred-mile voyage to Athens. Silas and Timothy remained in Beroea to help organize and strengthen the new church. Only Paul, who had done the preaching, was forced to flee.

The Life of Saint Paul

Athens is one of the world's most beautiful cities. What must it have been when Paul was there! To be sure, the Parthenon, temple of the goddess Athena, was then nearly five hundred years old, but high on the Acropolis it crowned the city with glory. All this marvelous display of temples, statues, and architectural vistas meant to Paul not so much beauty as idolatry. What endless gods and goddesses the Athenians worshiped! And lest they should miss any, they even erected an altar inscribed, "To an unknown god." This stirred Paul's imagination. Standing before a crowd of Athenians, he cried: "What therefore you worship as unknown, this I proclaim to you." But while he spoke with persuasive tact and skill, they did not understand him. When he mentioned Jesus and the resurrection, they thought he was trying to introduce them to two strange deities. So Paul made little impression on Athens. Two converts are mentioned by name, but we know of no Athenian church which Paul founded. One suspects that Paul was in a disappointed and anxious mood when he left Athens for Corinth.

Paul Invades Europe

Ever since leaving Macedonia, he had been most eager to return. He was worried about the churches at Philippi and Thessalonica and Beroea. Then Silas and Timothy joined him in Corinth with the best of news. The churches were strong and flourishing. They were steadfast, confident, and unafraid. "We have been comforted about you through your faith," Paul wrote to the Thessalonians, "for now we live, if you stand fast in the Lord."

So Paul and his companions settled down in Corinth. Paul's first concern was finding work so that he could support himself. He was always careful about that. Even after his brief stay in Thessalonica he could write, "We worked night and day, that we might not burden any of you." In Corinth he fortunately found a family of tent-makers, Aquila and Priscilla, who were Christian Jews, and he went to live and work with them.

Corinth had the reputation of being one of the richest and wickedest cities in the Greek world. Paul was so challenged by it that he remained there a year and a half. He started his missionary work in the synagogue, but he was soon rejected there. Whereupon he left the synagogue, saying, "From now on I will go to the Gentiles."

One very important Jewish convert was Crispus, the head man of the synagogue, who with all his family joined the Christian church. This conversion must have deeply angered the orthodox Jews in Corinth. Paul had stolen their outstanding man. They watched for a chance to destroy this troublesome preacher of a new faith, and they thought that chance had come when Gallio, a new Roman pronconsul, arrived at Corinth. The elders seized Paul and haled him before Gallio, charging that the apostle was persuading men to worship God in unlawful ways. Even before Paul spoke in self-defense, Gallio told the accusers that if Paul were suspected of crime the proconsul would listen to the charge. But since the accusation had to do with religious differences and the Jewish law, Gallio refused to be a judge. Though he probably did not believe in what we call the separation of church and state, Gallio's decision seems very close to that principle. His response evidently pleased the Greek crowd, for they seized Sosthenes, the new ruler of the synagogue, and gave him rough treatment. Gallio paid no attention.

Did this Sosthenes who led the attack on Paul in Gallio's court afterward become a Christian? The question is raised by the fact that months later, after Paul left Corinth and was writing his first letter to the church there, he began the letter with these words, "Paul . . . and our brother Sosthenes." We have no positive proof that this is the same Sosthenes who was beaten. But what a story if he really was the same man!

Paul found freedom in Corinth to carry on a prolonged ministry. One of the most important things he did was to write his two letters to the Thessalonians. Written only twenty years after the death of Jesus, they are the earliest writings in the New Testament. Paul could never have dreamed that nineteen centuries later those letters, translated into hundreds of languages, would be read by 800,000,000 Christians around the world. The frail rolls of papyrus were cherished by the Thessalonian church, copied and often reread, until at last they found their place in the complete New Testament.

VII

Paul at Ephesus

Why Paul left Corinth we are not sure. He had made a long stay there and had built a vigorous church. He had overcome his enemies and won his case in the Roman court. And, unlike his usual experience, he had not been forced to leave. But Paul was a pioneer. He dreamed of further conquests for Christ's cause, and this time his plans centered on the city of Ephesus, two hundred and fifty miles due east of Corinth across the Aegean

Paul at Ephesus

Sea. So one day, probably in the spring of A.D. 53, Paul and his company took ship in Cenchrea, the harbor of Corinth, and sailed east. The group included Aquila and Priscilla, who transferred their business of tentmaking to Ephesus.

In addition to being the capital of the province of Asia, Ephesus was the religious center of all Asia Minor. There, in all its glory, stood the great temple of the goddess Diana, or Artemis, which was acclaimed as one of the seven wonders of the world. It is reported to have been four times the size of the Parthenon in Athens. In the temple's shrine was a meteorite—"the sacred stone that fell from the sky," as *The Acts of the Apostles* puts it. Pilgrims thronged to this holy temple which was the business, as well as the religious, center of the city's life. One of the town's chief industries was the manufacture of little shrines, made of terra cotta, marble, or silver. The pilgrims dedicated these to the goddess or took them home as mementos. When Paul tackled Ephesus, he was tackling one of the most vigorous and successful exhibitions of paganism in the Roman world.

Although Ephesus was a Greek city, it also had a large Jewish population, and many of the Jews there had achieved Roman citizenship. We know this from the writings of Josephus, a Jewish historian of Paul's own time. The Jews of Ephesus must have been above the average in liberality and open-mindedness, for when Paul spoke in their synagogue they gave him an especially cordial welcome, asking him to come again and say more. He promised to return, "if God wills."

Having seen the difficult challenge and the appealing opportunity of that amazing city, Paul surely intended to return. But he had two other cities to visit before settling down in Ephesus. Almost three years had passed since he had seen the apostles in Jerusalem or his friends in Antioch. He wanted to keep the old ties strong with James and Peter, and also with his home church. So he took ship and sailed to Caesarea. From there he went up the Judean hills to the Holy City, visited the apostles there, and perhaps celebrated the Jewish feast of the Passover. Then he came back to Caesarea and sailed to receive a heart-warming welcome in Antioch.

The news which greeted Paul in Antioch, however, was not all cheerful. There was trouble in his dearly loved churches in Galatia. The men who insisted that everyone must become an orthodox Jew before he could become a good Christian were at work again. So Paul toured the Galatian churches once more, reassuring the troubled members and confounding his opponents. Then at last he returned to Ephesus, this time by land instead of by sea.

As Paul settled down for the longest mission he ever conducted in any one city, he began as was his habit with the synagogue. For three months he found a welcome there. Luke says that he "spoke boldly, arguing and pleading about the kingdom of God," and many responded to him. Then, however, the inevitable happened. Some of the Jews began seeing clearly that, while Paul himself was a Jew and while his gospel had its roots deep in Judaism, nevertheless he was preaching a new religion which was bound to split the synagogue. As Luke puts it, "some were stubborn and disbelieved." At last these foes made further work in the synagogue impossible for Paul. He rented instead a meeting place called "the hall of Tyrannus." There for two or three years he carried on his mission and established the most influential church he ever founded.

Paul faced in Ephesus not only the worship of idols like Artemis but also many popular superstitions that would seem strange to us. We think of magic as the clever ability to do tricks, and we hire magicians to entertain us. But in the Ephesus of Paul's day magic was taken with deadly seriousness.

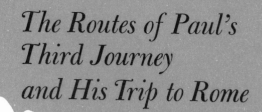

The Routes of Paul's Third Journey and His Trip to Rome

ITALY

Rome
The Three Taverns
Forum of Appius
Puteoli

MACEDONIA

Philippi
Thessalonica
Beroea

ACHAIA
(Greece)

Athens
Corinth

SICILY

Rhegium

Syracuse

MELITA
(Malta)

THE GREAT SEA
(Mediterranean)

LIBYA

—— THIRD JOURNEY
—— TRIP TO ROME

PONTUS EUXIMUS
(Black Sea)
THRACE
PAPHLAGONIA
GALATIA
PONTUS
Samothrace
ASIA
MINOR
Troas
Assos
Iconium
CAPPADOCIA
Aegean Sea
ASIA
Antioch
Mitylene
PISIDIA
Lystra
PAM-PHYLIA
Derbe
CILICIA
Ephesus
Tarsus
Samos
Miletus
Antioch
LYCIA
Patara
Cnidus
Myra
Cos
PHOENICIA
SYRIA
CYPRUS
CRETE
Sidon
Tyre
Ptolemais
PALESTINE
Cauda
Fair Havens
Caesarea
Jerusalem
ARABIA
Alexandria
EGYPT

Paul at Ephesus

All over that region many people relied for good luck and good health on charms written on papyrus. These were called "Ephesian papers." All sorts of folks, some doubtless sincere and some just plain rascals, made their living by casting demons out of people or promising them good fortune with the use of magic spells.

Paul's trouble began when he healed some men and women who were sick. Illness is often caused, as modern medicine well knows, not by disorder in the body but by disorder in the mind and emotions. Sometimes a powerful man like Paul can bring such sustaining faith, hope, and courage to people who need these qualities that they are restored to health. But the Ephesians thought that Paul was working magic, and they tried to profit by his mysterious spell.

Seven renegade Jews, who called themselves the sons of a high priest named Sceva, thought they would use Paul's magic. They made up a spell addressed to the demons which ran like this: "I adjure you by the Jesus whom Paul preaches." Unfortunately they tried their spell once too often. A deranged man on whom they were experimenting became violent. He leaped on them, knocked them down, and pummeled them, so that, as Luke says, "They fled out of that house naked and wounded."

The episode attracted wide attention, and some of the magicians confessed their crooked practices. As a result a great mass of their paper charms was burned in a public bonfire. All this, of course, helped to make Paul a public figure in the city.

During his mission in Ephesus, Paul worked hard at tentmaking, earning enough money not only to support himself but to help others. Then in the hall of Tyrannus he lectured and taught and organized a church. Alongside the Jewish converts, Gentiles began listening to him and responding to his appeal. We can sense how this thrilled him when he exclaims in a letter later written to the Ephesian church: "To me, though I am the very least of all the saints, this grace was given, to preach to the Gentiles the unsearchable riches of Christ."

As Paul's followers grew in number, news about him and about the gospel he preached spread throughout the region. The Roman province of

Paul at Ephesus

Asia was about the size of present-day New England. There were good roads, and throngs of pilgrims came to Ephesus for business or religious reasons. Soon Christian groups and churches sprang up all over the province. Converted Christians in Ephesus moved out to other towns. Or visitors to the city became Christians and carried the good news home with them. And then some one of Paul's helpers—Timothy, or Titus, or Erastus—went out to confirm the new churches. In the last book of the New Testament John, the author, sends messages to seven churches, all of them within easy reach of Ephesus. Almost certainly they all grew from seed which Paul planted.

Although the years which the apostle spent in Ephesus were thrilling, there were plenty of difficulties. He even wrote a letter to Corinth in which he said, "I die every day!" and "I fought with beasts at Ephesus." Since Paul, a Roman citizen, could not be literally thrown to the lions and tigers in the arena, this doubtless means simply that he faced desperate difficulties and dangers in his work. And one day the accumulating resentment against

Paul erupted into a dangerous, uncontrollable riot.

A man named Demetrius, a silversmith, started it. His business was making silver shrines, with an image of Artemis in each of them. Apparently he employed a considerable number of workmen, and he watched carefully to see whether the sales of his shrines were rising, keeping steady, or slipping. The longer Paul stayed in Ephesus and the stronger the Christian movement became, the more the sales of the silver idols slipped. The demand for shrines finally decreased until Demetrius could stand it no longer. He called his workmen together, along with other craftsmen, and made this speech to them:

Men, you know that from this business we have our wealth. And you see and hear that not only at Ephesus but almost throughout all Asia this Paul has persuaded and turned away a considerable company of people, saying that gods made with hands are not gods. And there is danger not only that this trade of ours may come into disrepute but also that the temple of the great goddess Artemis may count for nothing, and that she may even be deposed from her magnificence, she whom all Asia and the world worship.

Paul at Ephesus

That appeal to both pocketbook and patriotism started the riot. The crowd of craftsmen poured out into the street shouting, "Great is Artemis of the Ephesians!" Two friends of Paul, Gaius and Aristarchus, happened to be within reach. The crowd, joined by throngs of passers-by, seized them, and then the mob rushed together into the city's amphitheater, which seated twenty-five thousand people. Paul soon got word of the uproar and wished to go to the theater, but his fellow Christians would not let him. Even some of the city officials, wanting above all else to get the mob under control, begged him not to come. Meanwhile in the amphitheater all was wild confusion. Many of the crowd did not know what the turmoil was about, but if it involved the honor of their goddess they wanted to be counted on her side. A Jew named Alexander tried to speak to them, but they shouted him down. The Jews, like the Christians, were against idolatry and were hurting the city's business. So for two hours the mob crowded the amphitheater and shouted in an uproarious chorus: "Great is Artemis of the Ephesians."

Probably it was physical exhaustion which in the end quieted the crowd so that the town clerk —the most important official in the city—could address them. He presented four arguments to them. First, he said that they need not worry about Artemis, that she was invincible and that Ephesus, the keeper of her temple, was safe. Second, he said that no proper charge of disloyal conduct had been lodged against the Christians. They had uttered no blasphemy against the goddess. Third, he said that if Demetrius had been really wronged there were ample legal provisions by which he could secure his rights without inciting a riot. Fourth, he charged them with damaging the reputation of the city by their unruly rioting. So the mob dispersed, and Paul was free to stay in Ephesus.

Even before the riot, however, Paul had made up his mind that the time had come to go. Luke tells us that he had already made plans to visit Macedonia, Greece, and Jerusalem, adding, "After I have been there I must also see Rome." Paul had already sent Timothy and Erastus to visit churches in Macedonia, and he was putting the finishing touches on his work in Ephesus when the riot broke out. The uproar was a further argument for leaving, for his continued presence would almost certainly lead to more disturbance. So Paul's ministry in Ephesus came to a victorious conclusion in a prosperous church. The results of it continued long after the worship of Artemis ceased and her Ephesian temple crumbled and sank in the marshy plain.

VIII

Paul Heads for Jerusalem

When Paul left Ephesus he had three weighty matters on his mind. First, he was worried about the church in Corinth. One report after another, brought by travelers from Greece to Ephesus, had left no doubt that there was trouble among the Christians in Corinth. The Corinthian church had broken up into quarreling parties. There was dissension among the members which had even led to lawsuits in Roman courts. There had also been disorder in the services of public worship, and a few church members had interpreted liberty as meaning license and had been guilty of downright immorality.

Paul wrote them a long message which in the New Testament is entitled *The First Letter of Paul to the Corinthians.* It is an eloquent and moving appeal, with splendid passages in it such as the thirteenth chapter on love and the fifteenth on life eternal. The church in Corinth cherished and preserved the letter, and many of the members doubtless profited from it, but still it did not solve the problem. Some of the members resented the letter's stern rebukes, and apparently there was a ringleader, whose name we do not know, who organized opposition to Paul. Paul himself quotes the kind of thing his enemies in the Corinthian church said about him: "His [Paul's] letters are weighty and strong, but his bodily presence is weak, and his speech of no account."

Before leaving Ephesus, Paul wrote another letter. Scholars think we have that letter in chapters ten through thirteen of Second Corinthians. That is, they think that the New Testament book named

The Life of Saint Paul

The Second Letter of Paul to the Corinthians is made up of two, or perhaps three, different letters of Paul's which were preserved on the same roll of papyrus. Certainly chapters ten through thirteen fit perfectly the state of mind Paul was in when he left Ephesus. He was terribly upset. He could not bear losing the confidence and love of the church in Corinth. He must have handed this stormy letter to Titus, bidding him carry it to Corinth and do his best to win the church there to a better mind. Then he doubtless arranged to meet Titus at Troas to hear the news of what had happened.

The second concern which Paul had on his mind when he left Ephesus was anxiety about the collection of money. He was gathering contributions from all the churches he had founded to help the poor Christians in Jerusalem who were still suffering hard times. When Paul undertook anything, he put whole-hearted vigor into it. He was now determined to help the unity of the Christian churches by having the largely Gentile congregations contribute liberally to the Jewish congregation in Jerusalem. We do not commonly think of money-raising

Paul Heads for Jerusalem

as one of Paul's chief activities, but at this point in his life he was deeply concerned with it. Even today, when a church collection is being gathered for some good cause, the Scripture lesson is apt to be the eighth chapter of Second Corinthians. And Sunday after Sunday ministers announce the offering by quoting Paul: "God loves a cheerful giver." He was so in earnest about securing generous contributions from the churches that, even before the riot in Ephesus, he sent Timothy and Erastus ahead of him into Macedonia to speed up the offerings.

Paul's third concern, as he left Ephesus, was his growing conviction that he must go to Rome. Paul always worked in cities, and he could not leave out the capital city of the empire. Luke tells us that while Paul was still in Ephesus he planned the visit to Jerusalem and then said, "After I have been there, I must also see Rome." It was on this journey to Jerusalem, during his stop at Corinth, that he wrote his marvelous letter to the Romans, in which he says: "I have longed for many years to come to you; I hope to see you in passing as I go to Spain." Paul's adventurous spirit was unquenched. He pro-

posed to bring the gospel to the whole empire.
There already was a church in Rome, founded by
whom we do not know, and beyond Rome lay
Spain, one of the most prosperously developing
areas of all the imperial provinces. The prospect
captured Paul's imagination. He was determined to
visit both Rome and Spain.

So Paul sailed north to Troas. One imagines
him, as the ship docked, looking anxiously to see
if Titus was there to meet him. No Titus! What
could have happened to him? There had been time

enough for Titus to deliver the letter to the church in Corinth, to feel the church's response, to present Paul's case, and to keep the appointment at Troas.

A Christian group had been organized in Troas, and there was an open door for Paul to do some important missionary work. But he had no heart for it; he was worried. What was happening in Corinth, and where was Titus? After waiting as long as he thought wise, he took ship again and sailed for Macedonia. There, at Thessalonica perhaps, or Philippi, Titus came with the best of news. The Corinthian church had come over to Paul's side. The hostile ringleader had been disowned, and the members were sorry for the distress their misconduct had caused their founder. They were eager for Paul to visit them, and ready to show him their loyalty.

Paul rushed a letter off to them at once. Scholars think we have that letter in the first nine chapters of Second Corinthians. It certainly sounds that way. Read his outburst, as he begins the letter: "Blessed be the God and Father of our Lord Jesus

Christ, the Father of mercies and God of all comfort, who comforts us in all our affliction, so that we may be able to comfort those who are in any affliction, with the comfort with which we ourselves are comforted of God." Nine times in the first paragraph Paul mentions comfort. He had deeply needed it. As he wrote to the Corinthians about his previous letter: "I wrote you out of much affliction and anguish of heart and with many tears."

Now he could hardly wait to get back to Corinth. With a high heart he and his companions visited the Macedonian churches, encouraged the Christian work they were doing, and helped in collecting generous contributions for the Jerusalem church. Then Paul sailed for Corinth.

His coming must have been a joyful reunion. He stayed in Corinth for three months, and apparently the reconciliation was complete and the church was reunited. But Paul never could stay long out of danger. This time the peril came from the Jews in Corinth. We can readily understand why they hated Paul. He had taken some of the

Paul Heads for Jerusalem

most valuable members of their synagogue and had converted them to the Christian faith. And he valued very lightly many of the laws and ceremonies which the Pharisees held sacred. So when some of the Jews heard that Paul was sailing to Jerusalem on a ship that would also carry Jewish pilgrims to the Holy City, they thought they saw their chance. On shipboard they could get rid of Paul—perhaps throw him overboard—and none would be the wiser. Paul heard of the plot, however, and changed his plans. He took a ship going north and returned to Macedonia.

His change of plans had a most fortunate result. For this time, when Paul left Philippi, Luke came with him, and from then on to the end of his life was Paul's companion and physician. So once more *The Acts of the Apostles* stops being history told in the third person and becomes a personal diary. The change starts in Chapter 20, verse 6, where Luke writes, "*We* sailed away from Philippi . . . and in five days *we* came to them at Troas, where *we* stayed for seven days." One result of the record's thus becoming a diary is that we begin to read about very detailed incidents. For example, on the last night of their stay at Troas, the Lord's Supper was celebrated and Paul, so Luke says, "prolonged his speech until midnight." A young man named Eutychus was sitting on the window sill. Growing sleepy, he dozed off and fell from the window three stories to the ground. When his friends first reached him they thought he was dead, but Paul reassured them. In the end the youth recovered, and they all "were not a little comforted."

Then Luke continues his detailed diary, naming every port their ship stopped at—ten of them— until at last they reached Caesarea. To Paul the most moving incident of the voyage was undoubtedly the stopover at Miletus. It was only thirty miles, as the crow flies, from Ephesus, and Paul sent word to the elders of the Ephesian church, asking them to visit him. They came and their farewell meeting was very warm and affectionate. We think of Paul as one of the most towering and influential personalities in history, and he certainly was that. But in reading Luke's description of the way the Ephesian Christians said good-by to Paul

Paul Heads for Jerusalem

at Miletus, we can also feel what a friendly and lovable person he must have been. "They all wept and embraced Paul and kissed him," Luke records, "sorrowing most of all because of the word he had spoken, that they should see his face no more."

This note of sadness—that Paul was not coming back again, that something was going to happen to him—haunts that whole journey to Jerusalem. Paul himself felt that danger lay ahead, and even at Miletus he told his Ephesian friends "imprisonment and afflictions await me." At Tyre the Christians warned him not to go to Jerusalem. At Caesarea a Christian named Agabus took Paul's girdle. With it he bound his own feet and hands as a sign, so he said, that the Jews in Jerusalem would bind Paul and deliver him to the Gentiles. His prediction frightened the disciples, and they begged Paul not to go on to the Holy City. He was adamant, however. "What are you doing," he cried, "weeping and breaking my heart? For I am ready not only to be imprisoned but even to die at Jerusalem for the name of the Lord Jesus." Then the disciples gave up their frantic endeavors to persuade him. As Luke reports, "We ceased and said, 'The will of the Lord be done.'"

Why were so many of Paul's friends afraid of what might happen to him in Jerusalem? Part of the reason, of course, was the hostility of the Jews who resented the growth of Paul's work, who hated the new religion as a heresy, and who thought of Paul as a traitor to the Jewish faith. But that was not all. In the background was another fact which affected the whole life of Palestine. The Jews were seething with rebellion against Rome. Fear, suspicion, hatred, and violence were rampant and anyone like Paul, known to be friendly with Gentiles, was certainly in peril.

Even in Jesus' days, there had been Zealots, fanatical patriots who dreamed of a successful armed revolt against Rome. Josephus, the Jewish historian, who later wrote *The Wars of the Jews,* tells how this hope developed. By the time Paul made his last visit, the revolt had already reached the violent stage. Gangs of assassins, called Dagger-men, grew in number, and no man's life was safe if he was suspected of sympathy with the established order. Once an Egyptian Jew gathered an immense following on the Mount of Olives, planning to capture Jerusalem, but as in many similar cases the rebels were defeated with great slaughter.

Such was the Jerusalem to which Paul was going. No wonder his friends were anxious. His first welcome, however, was a friendly reception by the Christian fellowship. Paul and at least six companions brought with them a generous gift of money from the churches in the Gentile world. Of course this gesture of good will was appreciated. James and the other leaders of the Jerusalem church sincerely wished the Christian fellowship between Jews and Gentiles to be preserved. So Paul and his companions were warmly welcomed.

But to the faithful Jews Paul was a disloyal deserter who had betrayed Judaism to follow a false Messiah. And to many Christian Jews he was a suspected character who was teaching Gentiles that they need not observe Mosaic customs and ceremonies in order to be true disciples of Christ. He was even traveling with Gentiles, like Luke. Moreover, he was in the Holy City, which was seething with passionate resentment, both religious and political, against the Gentiles. He certainly was in danger.

So James and the other Jerusalem Christians suggested a plan which they thought might remove suspicion and hatred from Paul. He was to join a group of four Jewish Christians who had made a vow. When seven days had passed, the vow required them according to custom to shave their heads and purify themselves in a ceremony in the temple. The sight of Paul thus observing a Jewish ritual in the temple, so James hoped, might make the Jews think that Paul was not so bad a heretic after all. Paul consented to the plan, but alas! it did not work. Some Jews from Asia, who knew very well what Paul really believed and stood for, saw him in the holy place and raised a riot.

IX

Dangerous Days

It is not difficult to imagine what happened when the angry crowd in Jerusalem seized Paul. His enemies had undoubtedly been keeping a suspicious watch on him. Pilgrims from Europe and Asia were in the city to celebrate Pentecost, and many of them knew Paul's reputation as a betrayer of the Jewish faith. Some even recognized his Gentile companions—Trophimus from Ephesus, for example. Therefore when they saw Paul entering the sacred Court of Israel in the Temple, accompanied by Christian Jews and perhaps others, they raised an uproar. "Men of Israel, help!" they shouted. And then they cried out that Paul was an enemy of the Jews, that he taught men not to observe the Mosaic laws, and that he had defiled the holy place by bringing Gentiles—Trophimus in particular—into it.

This last charge was certainly false. Death was the penalty for any Gentile who entered the forbidden Court of Israel, and signs in Greek and Latin were posted to make the prohibition plain. A mob, however, takes rumors for facts and the enraged crowd, growing in numbers and ferocity, seized Paul and dragged him out of the Temple down the steps into the Court of the Gentiles. There, Luke tells us, they tried to kill him.

Fortunately for Paul the Roman barracks were located in the Castle of Antonia, a fort and headquarters of the Roman soldiers directly on the northwest corner of the Temple area. Two flights of steps led from Antonia to the Temple, and watchmen were constantly on guard, keeping a

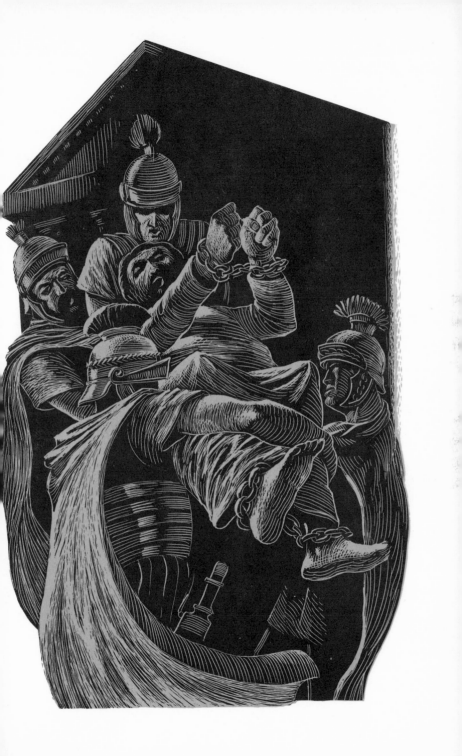

careful eye on what was happening. So when the riot broke out in the Court of the Gentiles, word swiftly reached the Roman tribune. With his soldiers he rushed to the scene of the trouble. When they appeared, the mob ceased beating Paul. The Roman tribune, who was acting not out of any sympathy with Paul but simply to stop the riot, arrested Paul and ordered him bound with two chains. Then he asked the crowd who Paul was and what he had done. Of course, the tribune got no clear answer. Some shouted one thing and some another until at last, seeing that he could get nowhere with the mob, the tribune ordered the prisoner to be taken to the barracks. So great was the crowd's violence that the soldiers actually had to carry Paul until they reached the steps of Antonia. From there they could look down on the rioters, who were shouting, "Away with him!"

Then Paul had an idea. Looking down on the howling mob that was shouting insults and threats at him, he thought: What an audience! What if I could make them listen to me? So, bruised and beaten though he was, Paul said to the tribune in

Greek, "May I say something to you?"

The tribune was astonished. "Do you know Greek?" he exclaimed. He had been thinking that Paul was probably the Egyptian rebel who had led the revolt in which the Romans slew thousands of his followers. Paul told the tribune that he was not the Egyptian but a Jew. And when Paul added, "I beg you, let me speak to the people," the astonished tribune consented.

So Paul motioned with his hands and, as the crowd grew quiet, he started speaking to them in Aramaic, the familiar Hebrew dialect which they all knew. "Brethren and fathers," he began, as though he were talking to a company of friends. Then he told them about his life as a faithful Jew, about his education under Gamaliel, about his zeal in strictly observing the law, and about his persecution of the Christians. No wonder that the crowd grew more and more quiet.

Then Paul moved out onto more dangerous ground and described his conversion on the Damascus road. As he went into detail about his marvelous experience there, hearing the voice of

the risen Christ, one suspects that there was rest-lessness in the crowd. But the explosion came when at last he mentioned his divine commission to go to the Gentiles. He never got beyond that hated word. The mob went wild. Luke tells us that they shouted, "Away with such a fellow from the earth! For he ought not to live." So the tribune, seeing the riot beginning again, hustled Paul into the Castle of Antonia.

There was something behind all this public dis-order which the Roman officer could not understand. How was he to find out? In characteristic Roman fashion he ordered Paul to be scourged. *That* would make him reveal the real secret of the trouble! But Paul, as he was being tied with thongs, put a stop to that plan by asking, "Is it lawful for you to scourge a man who is a Roman citizen, and uncondemned?" Of course it was not. So the tribune went to bed that night a very puzzled man. Luke even says that he "was afraid." How was he going to solve the mystery of this strange man, Paul?

When morning came, however, the Roman had a plan which seemed likely to succeed. He commanded the Jewish council to meet. Surely, he thought, they could explain to him whether Paul was a lawless troublemaker or an innocent man mistreated by the mob. The council was composed of leading Jews—priests who were Sadducees and a still larger group of Pharisees. What the tribune probably did not know was that on one point the Sadducees and the Pharisees sharply disagreed. The Pharisees believed in life after death, and they believed it in terms of the resurrection of the dead, while the Sadducees denied life after death.

No doubt the question of the resurrection of the dead came up soon after the meeting of the council began. Perhaps Paul, to whom Christ's continued life was so real, spoke of it. Certainly the subject was introduced and Paul, sensing the disagreement between the two parties in the council, saw his chance. "Brethren," he cried, "I am a Pharisee, a son of Pharisees; with respect to the hope and the resurrection of the dead I am on trial." Of course, from the standpoint of his Jewish foes that was not at all what he was on trial for. But from Paul's point of view, with Christ's resurrection central in his faith, that was the heart of the matter. At any rate Paul's strategy worked. The Sadducees and the Pharisees began quarreling. "A great clamor arose," says Luke. Some of the Pharisees even defended Paul while the Sadducees attacked him; until at last the scene became so violent that the tribune ordered the soldiers to take Paul back to his cell.

That tribune must have been a perplexed and baffled man. What was he to do with Paul? Then something happened which decided the matter. More than forty of the Jews took an oath that they would not eat or drink anything until they had killed Paul. They were probably Daggermen, who believed conscientiously that assassination was a justified way of destroying all those whom they regarded as enemies of Judaism. Having taken their dreadful oath, they went to the chief priests and elders and asked them to request the tribune to bring Paul down for another conference. The Daggermen promised that they would spring an ambush on Paul and kill him as he came to the meeting.

What saved Paul from this plot? Luke tells us that Paul had a nephew living in Jerusalem. Somehow or other the young man heard about the conspiracy against Paul's life. The fact that he did learn about it would indicate that he was considered a loyal Jew, certainly that he was not a Christian. But his conscience and his family loyalty would not allow this deadly plot against his uncle's life to succeed. First he visited Paul in the Castle of Antonia and told him about the proposed am-

136

bush. Then, at Paul's suggestion, he sought a secret interview with the tribune and told him. That settled matters. Paul was too difficult a problem for a tribune to handle. He must be sent to Caesarea to be dealt with by Felix, the Roman governor. So that night, at nine o'clock, with two hundred foot soldiers, seventy horsemen, and two hundred spearmen as an escort, Paul started on the sixty-mile journey to the Roman headquarters in Caesarea.

Felix, the governor, had been born a slave and had become a freedman. The fact that with such an unpromising start he had become governor of Judea shows that he was a forceful and ambitious character. He had a bad reputation, however, with both the Jews and the Romans. The Jews hated him for his brutality and Tacitus, the Roman historian, says that "he reveled in cruelty and lust, and wielded the power of a king with the mind of a slave." Nevertheless, he apparently greeted Paul kindly, saying that he would attend to his case as soon as Paul's accusers came from Jerusalem.

Five days later the accusers came, headed by

137

Ananias, the high priest. One can be sure that Paul and Ananias were not glad to see each other. At the meeting of the Jewish council in Jerusalem they had had an angry clash. Paul had said something which Ananias disliked and he had ordered a man standing by to strike Paul on the mouth. Paul had exploded. "God shall strike you, you white-washed wall!" Now the two faced each other again. How little they knew what lay ahead—Paul to become a martyr and a saint, and Ananias ten years afterward to be assassinated by his own people and his home burned down.

While Felix listened, Paul's accusers brought three charges against him: first, that he was a disturber of the peace among Jews everywhere; second, that he was a leader of the Christians; third, that he had defiled the temple. Paul's defense was fourfold: first, that his accusers had not proved him to be a troublesome insurrectionist; second, that it was not illegal to be a Christian; third, that he did not profane the temple and that no witnesses were present to testify that he did; fourth, that the council in Jerusalem had found nothing against

him. As Luke relates the hearing before Felix, the governor had no justifiable reason for keeping Paul a prisoner. But Felix was crafty and scheming. He wanted if he could to please the Jews. He postponed the whole affair by saying that he would decide the case when he had a chance to talk it over with the tribune from Jerusalem.

So began more than two years of imprisonment for Paul in Caesarea. To be sure, he seems to have been well treated. The Roman headquarters in Caesarea were in Herod's old palace, and it was there that Paul was kept in custody. He was always under observation by a guard, but his friends were allowed freely to visit him and minister to his welfare. Most of the companions who had come with him on the journey to Jerusalem naturally had to return home. But certainly Luke and probably Timothy and Tychicus remained within reach, and were of endless comfort to him.

Paul evidently interested Felix. Several times the governor summoned the prisoner to appear before him, and let Paul speak about his Christian convictions. Once the governor's wife, Drusilla—a beautiful nineteen-year-old Jewish princess of the house of Herod—was present, and Paul spoke with such force and challenge that Felix was alarmed.

"That will do for the present," he said to Paul. "When I have an opportunity I will summon you again."

Luke even says that Felix was hoping for a bribe from Paul. At any rate the months dragged by with no final judgment on Paul's case.

Then the blow fell, not on Paul but on Felix. As governor of Palestine his troubles had been growing. The determination of the rebellious Jews to escape from Roman tyranny was every year becoming more fierce and violent. The Daggermen in the cities and the roving bands of guerrilla rebels in the country made the maintenance of order increasingly difficult. Felix responded with more and more brutal measures of repression. Then came a fateful climax: violence broke out in Caesarea itself. A Jewish mob staged a demonstration. They were trying to drive out the Syrians and Greeks and take possession of the whole city for themselves. Felix struck hard with his Roman soldiery. The Jews were slain in large numbers and, as a result, an indignant protest blaming Felix was sent from Jerusalem to Rome. Rome wanted peaceful relations with its subject peoples. Having doubtless heard before that Felix was hated by the Jews, Nero the emperor dispossessed him, and appointed Porcius Festus governor in his place.

Festus wanted to be on good terms with the Jewish leaders, and the first thing he did was to make a friendly trip to Jerusalem. The Jewish leaders immediately demanded that Festus send Paul up to Jerusalem to be tried. Even after two years Paul's enemies were determined to do away with him. Festus, however, ordered a hearing for Paul—not in Jerusalem but in Caesarea. Once more his accusers attacked him, and once more he made his defense. Like Felix, Festus was puzzled. What did these differences between two kinds of Jews mean to him? He evidently saw nothing to justify the punishment of Paul on such charges as defiling the temple or endangering the empire by teaching that Jesus was the Messiah. Wanting to please the Jews, however, Festus asked Paul whether he was willing to be taken to Jerusalem for trial. Paul knew well that that would mean death. He had only one choice. Every Roman citizen had the right to appeal from a local court to Caesar's court in Rome. Paul had long said that he was going to see Rome, and here was one way of achieving his purpose. He could go to Rome as a prisoner.

"I appeal to Caesar," he said to Festus. That settled the matter. Paul would now be sent to Rome to be tried by the imperial court.

Before he sailed one interesting incident occurred. King Agrippa II and his sister Bernice came over from Galilee, where their royal home was, to pay a welcoming visit to the new governor of Judea. They both were Jews, and Festus told his visitors about Paul's perplexing case. Agrippa was interested, and so one day in the audience room of Herod's old palace Agrippa, Bernice, Festus, and doubtless many of their retinue heard Paul speak. He spoke at length, rehearsing once more the story of his early life and his conversion, and the audience listened attentively. Finally he began to pro-

144

claim his Christian faith, saying that all that Moses and the prophets had taught had been fulfilled in Jesus.

But when Paul began to declare that Jesus, crucified and risen again, would bring light to Jews and Gentiles alike, Festus interrupted him. "Paul, you are mad," he said. But Paul insisted on the truth of his gospel, and appealed to Agrippa to confess that it was so. Agrippa politely brushed Paul aside. "In a short time," he said, "you think to make me a Christian!" Both Festus and Agrippa were agreed that Paul must be sent to Rome for trial in Caesar's court.

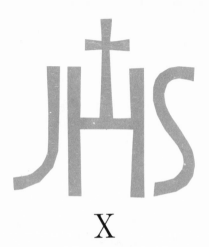

X

The Voyage to Rome

For some reason—perhaps because no ship was available—Paul's departure for Rome was delayed. That delay proved to be costly. From November to March the Mediterranean Sea was a rough and dangerous place for the sailing ships of Paul's day. For the most part navigation ceased during that time of the year. Paul's party sailed in September, a risky starting time since their ship was headed north along the Asian coast, in the hope of finding

The Voyage to Rome

another ship that would take Paul on to Italy.

Paul had two friends with him, Luke and Aristarchus. They probably were listed as his servants, or even slaves, in order to secure under Roman custom the privilege of accompanying him, a prisoner. A group of prisoners was on board, and a Roman officer named Julius was in charge of them and their guards. Julius evidently held a high opinion of Paul even from the beginning. At their first stop, Sidon, he gave Paul shore leave to go into the city and visit his Christian friends.

Contrary winds made the going difficult, but they beat their way up the coast until at last they reached a seaport named Myra, where they found a ship that was sailing for Italy. The transfer was made, and Paul found himself on a vessel carrying grain from Egypt to Rome. There were many such grain ships, for Rome depended on food from Egypt to feed its people. Evidently this vessel was a large one. Luke writes that there were 276 people on board. That certainly is possible, for Josephus tells us that he sailed for Rome on a grain ship that carried 600 people. From paintings, and engravings on coins, we know what those old sailing ships looked like. There was one main mast rising almost from the center of the hull, with a large square sail hung from a long spar attached at right angles to the mast's top. Then there was a small foremast, like an elongated bowsprit, which jutted out over the prow. There was no rudder such as we use, but two large paddles projected from the stern, one on each side. A rowboat was towed along behind for making shore landings.

Long before this journey, Paul had written to the Corinthians: "Three times I have been shipwrecked; a night and a day I have been adrift at sea." Therefore he must have foreseen their danger as the ship sailed along the Asian coast to a port named Cnidus, making the port with difficulty against rough seas and adverse winds. The ship's owner and the captain probably were hoping to make a straight course to Italy by passing to the north of the island of Crete, but the tempest was too much for them. It drove them to the south of Crete, where they hugged the coast to find some shelter from the wind. At last they reached a

harbor called Fair Havens and anchored there. A council was called to consider what they should do next. Some—Paul among them—advised that they spend the winter months in Fair Havens.

"Gentlemen," said Paul, "I see that the voyage will be with injury and loss not only to the cargo and the ship, but also to our lives." But the ship's owner and the captain thought otherwise. Fair Havens, they said, was a poor harbor for wintering. About thirty miles farther along the coast there was a much better port called Phoenix. As soon as the weather was more favorable, they would sail there and establish winter quarters.

One day a mild wind from the south sprang up. So, weighing anchor, they started for Phoenix. They never got there. Before the ship could cover those thirty miles the weather changed violently. Down from the mountains of Crete, which towered more than 7,000 feet above the sea, a "northeaster" roared upon the ship. It is easy to picture what happened to Paul's vessel—the ship's boat swamped, the sail and the mast under heavy strain and in danger of giving way, the hull beginning to leak, and the seamen unable to do much more than let the wind blow the ship where it would.

Then fortune favored them. They found themselves running into quieter water under the shelter of a little island called Cauda. Hauling the ship's boat out of the sea, they fastened it on the ship's deck. Then they put ropes around and under the ship and so undergirded her that she was in less danger of going to pieces. This done, they lowered the sail, so that only a small portion of it would catch the wind, and thus they reduced the strain on mast and canvas.

All these precautions made their situation safer, but their real troubles still lay ahead. The storm grew worse and worse. The next day they began lightening the ship by throwing overboard what they could safely spare—tackle, furniture, cargo. For two weeks they were driven helplessly by the tempest. They saw neither sun nor star, and having nothing like our modern compasses they had no idea where they were. They lost all hope. Their morale collapsed and they expected nothing but death.

The Voyage to Rome

Then Paul, with his indomitable bravery, breathed courage into them. "Gentlemen," he said, "you should have been persuaded by me not to start from Crete and to avoid this injury and loss. Now I advise you to be cheerful, for there will be no loss of life among you, but only the ship." Then he went on to share with his fearful fellows his conviction that they would all survive the storm. Paul habitually was at his best when the situation was at its worst.

On the fourteenth night after leaving Cauda, excitement swept through the ship. Those on board could hear something new—like storm-driven waves crashing on a shore. They became more and more sure of it. At once they made soundings to discover the depth of the water—twenty fathoms. Then they made another sounding —fifteen fathoms. That proved it: the ship was nearing a shore. The crew cast out four anchors from the stern to prevent the vessel from crashing into a possibly rugged coast. Then the ship's party prepared to wait until morning before attempting to land.

But the sailors had suffered all that they could stand. Fearing that the ship would break up, they selfishly plotted to desert the others. They lowered the ship's boat back into the water, saying that they were going to use it to lay anchors from the bow. Luke says that it was Paul who saw through their plot and told Julius and the soldiers about it. The sailors' plan to escape in the boat was thwarted. The soldiers cut it loose, and it drifted empty toward shore.

Meanwhile Paul was busy raising the morale of his fellow travelers. "Have something to eat," he said. "No one is going to be lost, but there will be hard work to do." He took bread and, after giving thanks, began to eat. "Then," writes Luke, "they were all of good cheer and themselves also took some food." They were sorely in need of it by this time.

When daylight came, the men saw that their ship was still anchored from the stern, her bow pointed toward a beach, while the tempestuous waves battered her from behind. They had already lightened the ship by throwing the cargo of grain overboard, but still there was a question of what would happen when they cut the anchor ropes and drifted onto the land.

What did happen was an unexpected shock to their hopes. They pulled in the rear anchors and got out the steering paddles, allowing the ship to be blown toward the beach. But between them and the beach was an underwater mud bank. The ship rammed into it, so that the prow was held fast and the stern began breaking up under the pounding of the waves. The frantic soldiers, fearing that some of the prisoners would jump overboard and escape, proposed killing them all. But Julius, "wishing to save Paul," according to Luke's account, forbade it. Instead the order was given that all who could swim should take to the sea and try for the beach. The rest were to try to get there on planks and pieces of the ship. Paul turned out to be right: everyone reached shore safely.

They soon found that they were on an island called Melita—now known as Malta. It lies about fifty miles south of Sicily, which is close to Italy. After leaving Cauda, the ship had drifted nearly

500 miles before the shipwreck. (Nowadays the visitor to Malta will be shown Saint Paul's Bay, the traditional site of his landing. Every bit of the shoreline corresponds with Luke's story, from the reef where the party first heard the breakers to the beach where they landed.)

It was raining and cold that morning, and the men's first need was for bonfires to warm them up and dry them out. The natives of Malta proved to be most friendly and hospitable. They straightway kindled fires and welcomed the wet and weary

The Voyage to Rome

strangers. Then once more Paul found himself in the limelight. As he was bringing in an armful of sticks for the bonfire, a poisonous viper bit his hand. The native Maltese at once began whispering to one another that Paul must be a murderer or some kind of criminal whom the goddess of justice was killing by snake's poison since he had escaped alive from the shipwreck. Paul, however, flipped the viper from his hand into the fire and went on with his work unharmed. Seeing after a long time that he was still alive and well, the whisperers changed their opinion completely. "He is a god," they said.

Then the chief man of the island, Publius, whose estates were near by, heard of the shipwreck. Most hospitably he took the stranded visitors in and cared for them three days. Meanwhile Julius, the Roman centurion, made plans to spend the rest of the winter on the island. He had had enough of the Mediterranean in winter, and for three months his whole party remained on Malta, waiting for the spring sailing season to begin. But one may be sure that Paul was not idle. How many people became Christians because Paul was shipwrecked on Malta one can only guess. But Luke, himself a physician, tells of some whom Paul cured of various illnesses. Publius' father was one of them.

When navigation began again they boarded a grain ship which had wintered in Malta. Stopping briefly at Syracuse in Sicily and at Rhegium, their first Italian port, they finally reached Puteoli on the beautiful bay of Naples. The rapid spread of Christianity in the Roman empire is indicated by the fact that in Puteoli Paul found a Christian fellowship. Then, when he started north by land, Christians from Rome met him at the Market of Appius, forty-three miles from their homes. And at The Three Taverns, ten miles farther north, another group from the Roman church greeted him. So although Paul was a prisoner he received a royal welcome; and when he reached Rome we may be sure that Julius gave him an excellent recommendation, for he was allowed to hire his own lodging, quite apart from the military encampment. There he lived with a guard but with

The Voyage to Rome

wide liberty, free to invite to his home anyone whom he pleased. Moreover, Epaphroditus came to Rome from Philippi, bringing a generous contribution of money from the church there to meet Paul's needs. So Paul settled down in Rome for at least two years.

At this point it is important to remember that it was not the Romans who had brought charges against Paul. It was his Jewish foes in Jerusalem who had accused him of disturbing the peace, and had prosecuted the case against him, first in the Holy City and then in Caesarea before Felix and Festus. The critical question which faced Paul in Rome was whether his enemies in Jerusalem would send representatives to Rome to continue the prosecution. One of the first things he did in Rome, therefore, was to call together the local leaders of the Jews and tell them his side of the story. They said that no news about him had come to them from Jerusalem and that no visitors from there had spoken evil of him. So the case rested, and Paul waited. But he was busy. "Friends," he wrote to the Philippians, "I want you to understand that

159

the work of the Gospel has been helped on, rather than hindered, by this business of mine. My imprisonment in Christ's cause has become common knowledge to all the imperial guard, and indeed among the public at large; and it has given confidence to most of our fellow Christians to speak the word of God fearlessly and with extraordinary courage."

Then, when we are eagerly waiting to hear what finally happened to Paul, Luke fails us. The last sentence of *The Acts of the Apostles* tells us that Paul lived in Rome for two years at his own expense, a prisoner but "preaching the kingdom of God and teaching about the Lord Jesus Christ quite openly and unhindered." There Luke's story stops. But many urgent questions remain unanswered. Was there a trial? What happened? Was Paul acquitted and did he go to Spain as he had hoped? Or was he condemned? If so, how did he die? Luke gives us no answer, but here are some of the guesses that scholars have made in explanation.

Perhaps Luke intended to write three books: his

The Voyage to Rome

Gospel, telling the story of Jesus; The *Acts of the Apostles,* telling about the first days of the church and especially the missionary journeys of Paul; and a third book about Paul's martyrdom, Peter's ministry and the expansion of Christianity throughout the known world. It may be, some think, that this was his plan, which he was unable to complete.

With regard to what happened to Paul some think that at the end of two years he was released. No prosecutors came, they suggest, and two years was the limit for holding a prisoner who had appealed to Caesar. Certainly at one time in his imprisonment Paul thought he was going to be released. Even in his letter to the Philippians, where he sometimes despairs, he writes of his hope of seeing his friends again. "I trust in the Lord that shortly I shall come also." Or read Paul's letter to Philemon, the shortest and one of the most fascinating manuscripts in the Bible. Philemon, a friend and perhaps a convert of Paul's had a slave named Onesimus. Onesimus stole money from his master, ran away, and at last reached Rome, where he heard about Paul's presence.

Having met Paul in Philemon's home, Onesimus called on him. Onesimus was converted to Christianity and he went back to Philemon, carrying this letter from Paul. Paul appeals to Philemon to forgive Onesimus, to receive him "no longer as a slave but more than a slave, as a beloved brother." Then Paul promises to pay any money that Onesimus owes, and he adds, "Prepare a guest room for me, for I am hoping through your prayers to be granted to you." So, some think, Paul was released. Perhaps he went to Spain, visited his beloved churches, and then was arrested again and taken to Rome for a second imprisonment.

Many, however, think that there was only one Roman imprisonment. In its earlier part, they say, Paul was hopeful of release. But then the prospects darkened and death became more and more certain, so that at last Paul wrote in his second letter to Timothy: "I am already on the point of being sacrificed; the time of my departure has come; I have fought the good fight, I have finished the race, I have kept the faith."

Whatever may be the facts about Paul's Roman

164

The Voyage to Rome

imprisonment and trial, there is no doubt about the final end. The tradition of the church from early days is unanimous about his martyrdom. He was beheaded on the Ostian Way, at a place of execution about three miles outside Rome. As a Roman citizen he could not be thrown to the lions in the public arena, as many Christians later were. He had a right to choose beheading as the manner of his death. How little the executioner suspected that he was making a martyr of one of the noblest men who ever influenced history.

A few years after Paul's death, still in the first century, an eminent churchman named Clement wrote to the Corinthians: "Paul, having been a herald in the east and in the west, received the high glory of his faith. When he had taught righteousness to the whole world, and had come to the limit of the west, and had borne witness before rulers, he so departed from the world and went to the holy place."

Glossary

apostles—the twelve followers who were with Jesus during his ministry and whom He sent out to teach the gospel. The original twelve included: Andrew, Bartholomew, James the Greater, James the Less, John the Evangelist, Judas Iscariot, Jude (or Judas Thaddeus), Matthew, Peter, Philip, Simon, Thomas. Matthias later replaced Judas Iscariot. Paul came to be known as the Apostle to the Gentiles, though he was not one of the original twelve.

Aramaic—any of a group of Semitic languages and dialects which were spoken throughout the Near East in ancient times. Aramaic was commonly used by the Jews in Palestine at the time of Jesus. *See also* Semitic.

Calvary—the place outside Jerusalem where Christ, according to tradition, was crucified.

centurion—the commander in the ancient Roman army of a company (*century*) made up of about 100 men.

Christian—a follower of Christianity, the religion based on the teachings of Jesus Christ and a belief in his divinity.

convert—a person who changes his beliefs in the principles of one religion for those of another.

166

Glossary

Deuteronomy—the fifth book of the Bible; part of the Old Testament.

disciple—a name used to refer to any of the close followers of, and believers in, Jesus and his teachings. *See also* apostle.

elder—an older man of influence and authority, especially in a church or community.

Essenes—a small Jewish sect which lived in ancient Palestine at the time of Jesus. They led an austere, strict life, striving to avoid contact with anything worldly or impure.

Gentile—in ancient times a term applied to any people who were not Jews.

gospel—the teachings of Christ and the apostles. *Also* anything that is told or accepted as being completely true.

Gospels—the first four books of the New Testament (*Matthew, Mark, Luke,* and *John*), containing the accounts of Christ's life and his teachings.

Hebrew—a member of that branch of the Semitic race which was descended from the line of Abraham; an Israelite; a Jew. *Also* a Semitic language spoken by the ancient Hebrews before 100 B.C. and used today by the Jews of Israel. *See also* Semitic.

idol—an image of a god used as an object of worship.

Glossary

Jew—one of the Hebrew or Jewish people, descendants of Abraham. For more than 3,000 years Jews have been held together by a common faith and history, but there is no one definition of a Jew on which all Jews agree.

Judaism—the religious doctrines and rites of the Jews, based on the laws and teachings of the Hebrew Bible or Old Testament, and its interpretations. The chief doctrine or principle of Judaism is a belief in one God. Both Christianity and Islam are derived from Judaism, although there are many basic differences in beliefs and practices.

kosher—a Hebrew word applied to food considered clean and wholesome according to Jewish ritual. Such food must be prepared according to certain rules. For instance, orthodox Jews may eat only the flesh of certain animals killed in a specified way. Neither milk nor milk products may be eaten with meats. Meat killed by hunters is not to be eaten.

martyr—a person who is willing to suffer and sacrifice even his life rather than give up his religion or principles.

messiah—a name given by ancient Hebrews to the ideal king or savior who was to deliver the Jewish people. The prophets said that such a messiah would appear, bringing about a period

168

Glossary

of peace and justice on earth. Paul and the early Christians taught that Jesus was the expected Messiah, but the majority of Jews did not accept this teaching.

missionary—a person sent out to persuade people to accept the religion which he practices and represents.

Mosaic Law—the ancient body of law which, according to the Old Testament, was handed down to the Hebrew people from God by Moses.

New Testament—a part of the Bible. Its 27 books were produced by the early Christian church. They make up a record of the new *testament* or promises made by God to man, as shown in the teachings and experiences of Jesus and his followers.

Old Testament—the first part of the Bible. *Testament* is an old word meaning covenant or agreement, and the Old Testament sets forth the idea of a covenant between God and His people. It is also an account of their history to show how faithfully they followed the covenant. Together, the Old and the New Testaments form the Scriptures that are sacred to Christians. Jews accept only the Old Testament, which they call the Hebrew Bible.

orthodox—correct or sound in one's beliefs, especially religious beliefs.

orthodox Jew—one who strictly follows the original Jewish laws and traditions.

Passover—an annual Jewish feast in memory of the "passing over" of the Hebrew children in Egypt when God destroyed all the first-born children of the Egyptians. The name also refers to the passing over of the Israelites from slavery (in Egypt) to freedom.

Pentecost—a Jewish feast which occurs on the fiftieth day from the second day of Passover, or seven weeks after Passover. It is held as a thanksgiving for the harvest. *Also* a Christian festival celebrated on the seventh Sunday after Easter in memory of the descent of the Holy Spirit upon the apostles on the day of the Jewish Passover.

Pharisees—a Jewish sect, active in Jesus' time, which followed strict religious laws that went beyond those contained in the Bible. The Pharisees believed in the resurrection of the dead and disagreed bitterly with their rivals, the Sadducees.

prophet—a person who declares that his beliefs have been divinely revealed to him as a religious message or a warning for the future. One who speaks for God.

rabbi—a religious teacher and spiritual leader of the

Glossary

Jews. Originally rabbi was a title of respect given by Jews to a doctor or teacher of the Hebrew law.

Sadducees—an ancient Jewish religious sect who followed only the written law of the Hebrew Bible and refused to be bound by the interpretations known as the Oral Law. They did not believe in immortality and they were opposed to the Pharisees in their beliefs and customs.

Scripture, or Scriptures—the sacred writings of the Old and the New Testaments, or of either of them.

sect—a group regarded as turning aside or departing from an established or general religious tradition. *Also* a group of people following a particular religious faith.

Semite—a member of a group speaking one of the Semitic languages. The ancient Hebrews, Phoenicians, and Assyrians were all Semites. The Arabs are present-day Semitic-speaking peoples.

Semitic—an important family of languages which include Hebrew, Aramaic, Arabic, Syrian, and Phoenician. *Also* of or pertaining to the Semites or their languages.

synagogue—a Jewish house of worship. *Also* an assembly of the Jews for purposes of religious instruction and worship, apart from the service of the temple.

Index

172

Index

173

Index

Index